Contributors: James P. Hess — Ivy Tech State College    Chris Moore    Raymond — Central Conn. State Univ.

# Prentice Hall's Guide to e-commerce and e-Business

## 2001 Edition

### Marian Wood
Strategic Management Services

Upper Saddle River, New Jersey 07458

Development: *Melene Kubat, Audrey Regan,* and *Steve Deitmer*
Print Production Manager: *Christy Mahon*
Project Manager: *Theresa Festa*
Cover design: *Michael J. Fruhbeis*
Interior design: *Kim Easteadt, Black Diamond Graphics*

Copyright 2001 by Prentice Hall, Inc.
A division of Pearson Education
Upper Saddle River, New Jersey 07458

All rights reserved. No part of this book may be reproduced, in any form or by any means, electronic or mechanical, including photocopying, recording, or any information storage and retrieval system, without permission in writing from the Publisher.

Printed in the United States of America.

10 9 8 7 6 5 4 3 2 1

ISBN 0-13-027813-0

Screen shots reprinted with permission from the following companies and organizations:

FreeMarkets
FedCenter.com
eBay, Inc.
Snap.com, a service of NBC Internet, copyright 3/24/00 (www.snap.com).
Google
Metacrawler/Go2Net, Inc.
New York State Department of Labor
Monster.com
The College for Financial Planning, CPE*Internet*

The authors and publishers of this manual have used their best efforts in preparing this book. The authors and publisher make no warranty of any kind, expressed or implied, with regard to these programs or the documentation contained in this book. The authors and publisher shall not be liable in any event for incidental or consequential damages in connection with, or arising out of, the furnishing, performance, or use of the programs described in this book.

# What's Inside

Preface

**Chapter 1** — **Introduction to E-Business and E-Commerce**
- E-Business, E-Commerce, and the New Economy
- Components of E-Commerce
- E-Commerce Around the World
- Looking Ahead: Challenges and Opportunities
- E-Business and Marketing/Advertising
- E-Business and Management/Human Resources
- E-Business and Strategy
- E-Business and Finance
- E-Business and Legal Studies
- E-Business and Accounting
- E-Business and Economics
- E-Business and Business Communication
- E-Business and MIS
- E-Business and Decision Science

**Chapter 2** — **Searching the Internet**
- Subject Tree Search
- Open Text Search
- Advanced Search Techniques
- Go Beyond with Metasearch
- More Search Engines
- Evaluating and Using Search Results

**Chapter 3** — **Career Development on the Internet**
- How to Research Careers and Employers
- How to Find Job Openings
- How to Create an Electronic Résumé
- For Further Career Surfing
- Preparing for a Career in E-Business
- Additional Resources

**Chapter 4** — **Distance Learning on the Internet**
- What is distance learning?
- Advantages and Disadvantages
- A Distance Learning Sampler
- 10 Questions to Ask Before You Register
- Learning in Cyberspace

**Chapter 5** — **Business-Related Internet Addresses**

Glossary

Sources

# Preface

In the new world of business, you'll run into e-commerce no matter what direction you turn. Perhaps no one can accurately predict how business will look in the coming years -- it's changing every day -- but it seems certain that e-commerce will be an increasingly big part of it. For moving around in the e-business world, for searching out information, for looking for jobs, for continuing your education, the Internet seems destined to play a big role. This guide introduces you to many aspects of e-business and the Internet, as the following table of contents promises. We want you to have the tools to succeed in your courses and in the real world, whatever direction you choose to take.

## Chapter 1: Introduction to E-Business and E-Commerce
*An overview of the basic concepts of e-business and e-commerce.* This chapter provides background and perspective on the growth and importance of e-business. We introduce you to the new concepts emerging from the new ways of doing business on the Internet.

## Chapter 2: Searching the Internet
*An introduction to popular search sites and advanced search techniques for finding information on the Internet.* You also learn how to evaluate the credibility of an online source and how to avoid plagiarism.

## Chapter 3: Career Development on the Internet
*An up-to-the-minute look at online job searches and career sites.* We offer tips on how to prepare an electronic résumé, and we annotate hot online job sites. You will also learn about using Web-based self-assessment tools to prepare for a career in e-business.

## Chapter 4: Distance Learning on the Internet
*You will learn what questions to ask to ensure you're taking the right distance-learning course.* We also offer a student's-eye view of what taking a distance-learning course entails.

## Chapter 5: Business-Related Internet Addresses
*A wide range of URLs tied to the world of business.* These URLs -- for actual businesses, for academic sites, for student-success sites, and more -- will get you started on your Internet way.

## Glossary
*Key terms to help you speak the language of e-business.*

## Online Coverage
*Current-events updates, additional mini-cases, and interactive exercises posted on the Web.* Visit us at
**http://www.prenhall.com/ebiz**.

# Chapter 1
# Introduction to E-Business and E-Commerce

## E-Business, E-Commerce, and the New Economy

When the Internet was in its infancy—little more than a decade ago—words like *e-commerce* and *e-business* had not yet been invented. Now the Internet has become such an integral part of the business world that experts had to create a special phrase—the *new economy*—for its contribution to the economy. The *new economy*, also known as the *Internet economy*, consists of businesses that generate all or some of their revenues from the Internet or Internet-related goods and services.

Both e-commerce and e-business are part of the new economy. The exchange transactions that take place on the Internet (such as buying, selling, or trading goods, services, and information) are known as *e-commerce*. *E-business* is a broader term covering the combination of business processes, technology, and organizational structure needed for e-commerce.

E-businesses such as Yahoo! (**http://www.yahoo.com**) and Amazon.com (**http://www.amazon.com**) were e-commerce pioneers, attracting the public imagination with their ingenious presentations and innovative use of Internet technology. Yet some of today's most successful—and profitable—e-businesses aren't even "dot-coms" (Internet-based businesses). IBM (**http://www.ibm.com**) and Dell (**http://www.dell.com**) are two of the growing list of traditional firms that now use the Web to improve internal processes, boost sales, and satisfy customers.

## Components of E-Commerce

What comes to mind when you think of e-commerce? Amazon.com, perhaps? Well, e-commerce is much more than *e-tailers* (Internet retailers). It's made up of exchanges among businesses, consumers, and government agencies, which can be classified according to which party initiates and controls the exchange transaction and which party is the target of the exchange. Table 1 shows these components, along with a Web example of each.

## Table 1 – Classifying E-Commerce Sites

|  | **To Business** | **To Consumer** | **To Government** |
|---|---|---|---|
| **Initiated by Business** | Business-to-Business (B2B) FreeMarkets http://www.freemarkets.com | Business-to-Consumer (B2C) Amazon.com http://www.amazon.com | Business-to-Government (B2G) FedCenter.com http://www.fedcenter.com |
| **Initiated by Consumer** | Consumer-to-Business (C2B) Better Business Bureau site http://www.bbb.org/ | Consumer-to-Consumer (C2C) eBay http://www.ebay.com | Consumer-to-Government (C2G) GovWorks http://www.govworks.com/ |
| **Initiated by Government** | Government-to-Business (G2B) Small Business Administration site http://www.sba.gov/ | Government-to-Consumer (G2C) California state site http://www.state.ca.us/ | Government-to-Government (G2G) Fed Services site http://www.fedworld.gov/fedservices/fedworld/ |

In e-commerce jargon, *B2C* means business-to-consumer (initiated by a business, aimed at consumers) transactions, *B2B* means business-to-business transactions, and *B2G* means business-to-government transactions. Similarly, *C2B* means consumer-to-business, *C2C* means consumer-to-consumer, and *C2G* means consumer-to-government. Finally, *G2B* means government-to-business, *G2C* means government-to-consumer, and *G2G* means government-to-government. Here's a closer look at each of these e-commerce components.

**B2B**. Business-to-business transactions account for most of today's e-commerce sales volume, because they generally involve higher prices and larger quantities than B2C transactions. Within three years, B2B transactions could hit $4 trillion. Taking advantage of the speed and convenience of the Web, companies such as Cisco (**http://www.cisco.com**) now buy nearly all their supplies and sell many of their computer-related products online. The Internet makes business buying so efficient that British Telecom expects to save 11% by moving its purchasing to the Web. E-commerce volume is also growing at *B2B online markets*, Web sites that facilitate the exchange of goods and services among organizational buyers and sellers. One example is FreeMarkets (**http://www.freemarkets.com**), which auctions materials and components, supplies, and services in 70 product categories. See Figure 1.1. These B2B sites help participating businesses reduce buying costs, expand access to more suppliers, and slash the time and paperwork needed to complete purchases.

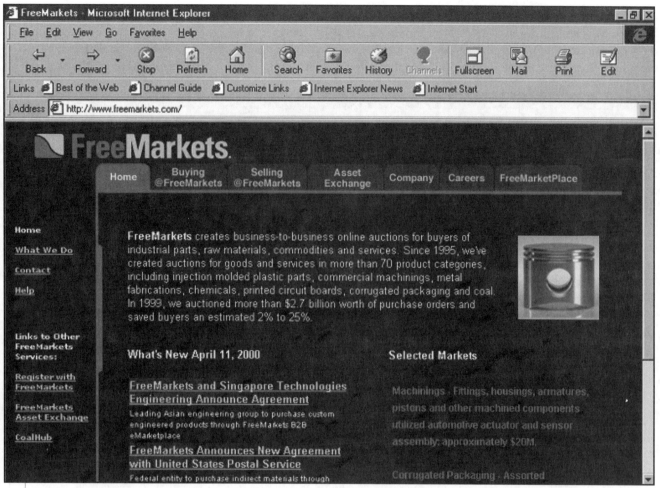

Figure 1.1 FreeMarkets is a B2B auction site that brings together business buyers and sellers of components and raw materials.

**B2C.** Although B2C transactions are a smaller part of e-commerce than B2B transactions, they are capturing an ever-larger share of all retail sales. By 2003, B2C could reach $400 billion in annual sales. Currently, most B2C transactions take place on five Web sites: Amazon.com, eBay (**http://www.ebay.com**), America Online, Yahoo! and Buy.com (**http://www.buy.com**). As this list indicates, dot-coms enjoy an early e-commerce lead over store-based retailers. Why? Barnes and Noble, like so many other firms, dragged its feet in starting an e-business unit (**http://www.bn.com**) out of fear that online sales would cut into the sales of the *legacy business,* the traditional, non-Internet business unit. Meanwhile, start-ups such as Amazon roared ahead, building their brands and their customer bases with aggressive marketing programs. By the time bn.com started clicking, Amazon was way ahead. Last year, bn.com rang up $202 million in sales, compared with Amazon's $1.6 billion in sales. Online competition is so fierce that as many as 25,000 of today's 30,000 e-tailers may ultimately be driven out of business.

**B2G.** Government agencies on the local, state, and federal level represent a huge and lucrative market for businesses selling all kinds of goods, services, and information. Government agencies purchase more than $77 billion annually in technology goods and services—and that's only the tip of the procurement iceberg, because it doesn't count non-technology purchasing. That's why B2G sites like FedCenter.com (**http://www.fedcenter.com**) are setting up shop on the Internet. See Figure 1.2. Once government buyers register at FedCenter and receive their passwords, they search the site for goods and services by category and then click to set the purchase in motion. FedCenter offers 3 million items—everything from office furniture to medical supplies—and government buyers can comparison-shop right on the site.

Figure 1.2. FedCenter.com is a B2G one-stop shopping site for government buyers seeking business products and services.

*C2C.* Consumer-to-consumer transactions are of lower dollar amounts and account for a far smaller piece of the e-commerce pie than B2B, B2C, or B2G transactions. Yet eBay (**http://www.ebay.com**) is one of the highest-profile sites on the Internet because so many people are hopping on the Internet auction bandwagon to buy and sell collectibles and other items online. See Figure 1.3. The name-your-price e-business Priceline.com (**http://www.priceline.com**) has also entered the C2C marketplace with its virtual yard sale, allowing individuals to buy and sell all kinds of new and used products—from boom boxes to baby carriages. Both eBay and Priceline charge sellers a small fee when items sell.

Figure 1.3. The eBay site is a C2C auction site that allows consumers (and some businesses) to buy and sell a wide variety of products.

***C2B.*** In consumer-to-business transactions the consumer, not the business, initiates and controls the exchange. One C2B site is Mob Shop (**http://www.mobshop.com**), formerly known as Accompany.com, a site that allows consumers to band together for volume discounts on electronics and other items offered by participating suppliers. Another C2B site, Respond.com (**http://www.respond.com**), lets consumers post requests for items they want to purchase so businesses can respond with specific offers. The private, nonprofit Better Business Bureau, funded by businesses, also operates a C2B site (**http://www.bbb.org/**). Consumers can search this Web site for free information about problems other consumers have reported with particular businesses, charities, and investment firms.

***C2G.*** One of the fastest-growing areas of e-commerce is C2G, which covers consumer-initiated transactions with government agencies. GovWorks (**http://www.govworks.com/**) lets consumers pay government agencies online for traffic fines, real estate taxes, and government licenses and permits. GovWorks makes money by charging consumers a service fee for each payment and by selling site sponsorships. Another C2G site, ezgov.com (**http://www.ezgov.com**), is signing agreements with state and local governments to accept online payments from consumers—again, with service fees paid by consumers. Both sites offer time-pressured consumers the convenience of making payments without having to wait in line at some government office.

*G2C.* More and more government agencies are establishing Web sites to provide information and services to consumers. As one example, the California site (**http://www.state.ca.us/**) contains pages of free data about state services, transportation, public safety, health care, state history, and much more. Some government sites, such as the Washington, D.C., site (**http://www.washingtondc.gov**), allow online transactions such as driver's license renewals as well as business transactions such as permit applications. In addition, Oregon and 11 other states have begun selling seized and surplus property to consumers through eBay auctions. For example, Oregon has sold sell hundreds of items on eBay, from tools to jewels. These state sales on eBay have been so successful that the federal government is now planning a separate auction site for its own G2C transactions.

*G2B.* Businesses are another constituency that government agencies want to reach online. The U.S. Small Business Administration site (**http://www.sba.gov/**), for example, is a G2B site offering information and financial assistance to small businesses. The site helps entrepreneurs learn how to establish a business, obtain funding for expansion, buy or sell overseas, and tap other government resources. A number of municipalities also maintain Web sites to solicit business bids on government purchases of goods and services. The Fort Collins, Colorado, purchasing site (**http://www.ci.fort-collins.co.us/city_hall/purchasing/**) lists current purchasing needs and offers downloadable documents for businesses to use in submitting bids.

*G2G.* Government-to-government transactions are much less visible to the public than other e-commerce components. One G2G site is the Government Agency Services page on the FedWorld site (**http://www.fedworld.gov/fed-services/fedworld/**), maintained by the National Technical Information Service (NTIS). The NTIS will help any other federal government information agency design a Web site, set up online procurement, sell publications online, or create a database—for a fee. Although this arrangement pits the NTIS against businesses that provide the same services, it also permits the NTIS to generate revenues and offset its operational costs.

## E-Commerce Around the World

U.S. consumers, businesses, and government buyers have been steadily increasing their online purchasing since the early 1990s—a trend that will only accelerate as more people and organizations log on to the Web. According to the U.S. Department of Commerce, U.S. consumers spent $5.3 billion on goods and services online during the last quarter of 1999, not including online travel purchases (which the government counts separately—$2 billion during that period). The top five product categories for online purchasing are computer hardware and software, travel services, securities investments, collectible items, and music, videos, and books. Meanwhile, U.S.-based giants such as General Electric (**http://www.ge.com**) and General Motors (**http://www.gm.com**) are saving money and time by shifting the bulk of their global business buying and selling to the Web.

The monetary value of European e-commerce is not yet at the U.S. level, but it is growing rapidly, fueled by fast-rising Internet usage, the shift to a single currency (the euro), and new wireless methods of Web access. Eyeing the opportunities, businesses such as Britain's Harrods department store (**http://www.harrods.co.uk**) are promoting their Web sites, even as U.S.-based firms such as E-Loan (**http://www.eloan.com**) launch European Web operations. Some European retailers, such as U.K. retailer Dixons (**http://www.dixons.com**), are even encouraging e-commerce by offering free Web access through their own Internet service provider (ISP) divisions. In fact, Dixons' Freeserve ISP has more users than the European version of America Online (**http://www.aol.com**).

E-commerce in Japan is growing more slowly than in the United States and Europe, because far fewer people own personal computers. Still, online purchasing is getting a boost from the wild popularity of wireless Internet access offered by NTT DoCoMo (**http://www.nttdocomo.com/**), the country's largest mobile phone operator. Teens wear the colorful DoCoMo phone like jewelry and use its voice-recognition technology to speed-dial friends and log on to participating Web sites. DoCoMo has already signed 6 million customers and is adding more than 25,000 new subscribers every day. Small wonder that telecommunications providers outside Japan are watching DoCoMo's Internet strategy with great interest.

## Looking Ahead: Challenges and Opportunities

What lies ahead for e-businesses? Here, categorized by business discipline, is a quick overview of key challenges and opportunities facing e-businesses in the new economy.

*Marketing and Advertising.* With so much competition from dot-coms and legacy businesses—and so many new opportunities to reach and satisfy customers—e-businesses are finding new ways of using the four Ps of the marketing mix (product, place, pricing, promotion) to build their brands online for competitive advantage.

*Management and Human Resources Management.* How can e-business managers plan, organize, lead, and control in the ever-changing Internet environment? Meeting this challenge, e-business managers are developing virtual organizations, adding corporate portals (internal Web sites), and offering employee-gripe Web pages. They're also becoming more creative in recruiting employees.

*Strategy.* E-commerce has created new challenges and opportunities for managers to consider as they craft strategy. A key challenge: Deciding whether to separate or integrate e-businesses and legacy businesses in the portfolio. A key opportunity: Using the Internet to deliver superior customer service as part of a differentiation strategy.

*Finance.* Where do e-businesses get the cash they need to set up shop and pay for marketing to attract and retain customers? Venture capitalists and for-profit incubators are common sources of financing. In addition, the Internet enables e-businesses to offer their stock to online investors.

*Legal Studies in Business.* Many e-businesses are taking legal steps to protect intellectual property such as Internet domain names and Web patents. Privacy online is another hot legal issue. Information is the lifeblood of e-commerce, yet many consumers and privacy advocates worry that too much personal data is too available on the Web.

*Accounting, Auditing, and Taxation.* The explosive growth of e-commerce has put the spotlight on key accounting, auditing, and taxation issues. When and how should an e-business recognize revenues? Should e-businesses capitalize or expense costs? And should Internet sales be taxed?

*Economics.* The Internet has opened new business opportunities in four areas: infrastructure, applications, intermediaries, and commerce. It has also cleared the way for cashless payment alternatives such as electronic cash and electronic barter—and for B2B online markets to facilitate the exchange of goods and services among organizational buyers and sellers.

***Business Communication.*** Writing for online readers is a major challenge for business communicators. With more than 569 million e-mailboxes around the world, e-businesses are also able to take advantage of new communication opportunities—if they steer clear of spam (unsolicited e-mail) and comply with rules governing specialized messages.

***Management Information Systems.*** E-businesses are using two types of private computer networks -- intranets and extranets -- to handle the challenge of supporting their e-commerce operations. And the Internet has led to new methods of obtaining specialized application software—as well as to new ways of enhancing online customer service.

***Decision Sciences.*** Sophisticated Internet-based technologies are creating new opportunities for e-businesses to more efficiently and effectively manage all the links in the supply chain. Not only are firms managing inputs by moving procurement to the Web—they're managing outputs by installing computerized systems to optimize production efficiency.

Let's turn now to a closer look at the new economy and these various business disciplines. And don't forget to check the Prentice Hall E-Biz Web site (**http://www.prenhall.com/ebiz**) for current-events updates, additional mini-cases, and interactive exercises.

---

## E-Business and Marketing/Advertising

### Building the Brand Today For Tomorrow's Profits

Before 1995, the word "Amazon" conjured up images of the South American river or female warriors. Today, Amazon.com (**http://www.amazon.com**), the Internet bookseller, is one of the best-known brands in online retailing. In just a few years, founder Jeff Bezos and his staff have built Amazon into the brand of choice for millions. Of course, brand equity doesn't necessarily translate into immediate profits, as Bezos has learned.

Brand building requires a long-term strategy incorporating product, promotion, pricing, and place to make more buyers aware of the brand and its value. Over time, as customers come to prefer the brand, become loyal users, and continue to buy, brand equity goes up—as does profitability. Here's how e-businesses are using the 4Ps to build their brands.

### Using Product to Build Brand Equity

A growing number of companies are building online brands using the site as the product. Look at the Internet battle between *Financial Times* and the *Wall Street Journal*. The free *Financial Times* site (**http://www.ft.com**) differentiates its online brand from its newspaper brand with shorter news stories, a business search engine, and other business links. In contrast, *Wall Street Journal Interactive* (**http://www.wsj.com**), with over 375,000 paid subscribers, posts the newspaper's printed stories online, links to other Dow Jones publications, and uses the newspaper's typeface to reinforce the brand.

In addition, unique or specialized products can build a brand. Hot Hot Hot (**http://www.hothothot.com**), a hot-sauce store in Pasadena, California, expanded to the Web to sell internationally. Hot products and fiery graphics are Hot Hot Hot's recipe for e-commerce success. Visitors can also sign up to receive e-catalog updates—a regular reminder of the brand and its value.

### Using Promotion to Build Brand Equity

More e-businesses are building brands with *viral marketing*, the use of e-mail messages that encourage recipients to send the message to others. Viral marketing circulates messages among people who know each other, unlike *spam*, unsolicited e-mail messages often sent out in bulk. Hotmail.com (**http://www.hotmail.com**) used viral marketing to become a top free e-mail brand. Every Hotmail message carries a simple tag: "Get your private, free email at **http://www.hotmail.com**." Like a virus, this message spreads from user to user—building the Hotmail brand and increasing the site's usage.

Viral marketing is building brands in other areas, as well. On Valentine's Day, online traffic at electronic greeting card sites skyrocketed 30% as recipients read their cards and rushed to send cards of their own. This is how Blue Mountain Arts (**http://www.bluemountain.com**) built its online brand into the industry leader, serving more than nine million users per month.

## Using Pricing to Build Brand Equity

Pricing is a popular Web branding tool. Consider how Reel.com (**http://www.reel.com**) built its brand through discounting. When the site offered the *Titanic* video at a special low price, it drew over 300,000 new customers and made its name as an online video brand. The most extreme use of pricing is to charge nothing, as when Netscape and Microsoft began giving away their Web browsers. Now Sun Microsystems is offering StarOffice software via free downloads (at **http://www.sun.com/staroffice**) to build the brand by enlarging the user base.

The Internet has ushered in a new era of *dynamic pricing*, which means prices change from transaction to transaction. The pricing strategy that built the eBay brand (**http://www.ebay.com**) is *auction pricing*, in which buyers bid against each other and the highest bidder buys the product. Priceline.com (**http://www.priceline.com**) built its brand through the *name-your- price strategy*, in which buyers state how much they will pay and suppliers decide whether to sell at that price. Mobshop.com (**http://www.mobshop.com**) is building its brand through *group buying*, in which the price goes down as more buyers band together to buy an item.

## Using Place to Build Brand Equity

Many e-businesses use place for brand building. For example, CarsDirect.com (**http://www.carsdirect.com**) lets buyers check vehicle information and order online. The brand name reminds customers that they can buy without going to a dealer—because the vehicle is delivered directly to the customer.

Convenient delivery is the main benefit of grocery delivery e-businesses such as Webvan (**http://www.webvan.com**). Customers log on, select products, then check out and select a 30-minute window for delivery. Webvan offers its services only in markets where it has a distribution center and a delivery fleet, because timeliness is key: Webvan says 98% of its deliveries are on time.

### ✔ E-Business Case in Point: Sears, Roebuck

Although Sears, Roebuck's roots are in the old economy, the retailer is finding new ways to wield its considerable brand equity on the Web:

- *Todo Para Ti*. Translated as "Everything For You," the company's Spanish-language site (**http://www.sears.com/todoparati**) is designed for Latino e-commerce shoppers in the United States as well as non-U.S. Latino consumers who buy at Sears when they visit.

- *BobVila.com*. With spokesperson Bob Vila, Sears is creating BobVila.com (**http://www.bobvila.com**), where do-it-yourselfers can find instructions for repair and construction projects and buy tools, supplies, videos, and books. The association with Vila helps strengthen brand equity for Sears products such as Craftsman tools.

- *GlobalNetXchange.* Sears is working with France's Carrefour (hypermarkets), Oracle (software), Britain's Sainsbury (supermarkets), and other partners to create a B2B (business-to-business) site where members can buy, sell, trade, or auction merchandise. When it comes online, this site should give the Sears brand a boost in B2B.

1. How could Sears use viral marketing to increase traffic to BobVila.com?
2. Why would Sears avoid using its brand on the GlobalNetXchange B2B site?

---

## E-Business and Management /Human Resources
### Managing on Internet Time
How can e-business managers plan, organize, lead, and control in an environment that changes every minute? Managing on Internet time requires speed, communication, and flexibility; e-businesses need to share information quickly and tap the talents of every employee, regardless of location, in the race to achieve their goals.

Consider a *virtual organization*, a structure in which people (employees and, sometimes, non-employees) in different locations use communication technology to work together. For example, 658 volunteer (non-employee) programmers all over the world form the virtual organization creating Fetchmail e-mail software (**http://www.fetchmail.com**). Many e-businesses are establishing *virtual teams*, using technology to link team members in different places with a *virtual team leader* to coordinate members' activities. How do e-businesses communicate with employees in virtual organizations?

### Communicating Portal to Portal
In many companies, communication travels via an *intranet*, an internal communication network. Now Intel (**http://www.intel.com**) and other companies have gone beyond the intranet by setting up a *corporate portal*, a comprehensive internal Web site with company information that employees can personalize and access as needed. Just as visitors to the Yahoo! portal (**http://www.yahoo.com**) can customize content using the "My Yahoo!" feature, corporate portals allow employees to personalize their pages.

Once employees log on, they can interact with other team members and share knowledge about projects within the organization. For example, BrightStar (**http://www.brightstar.com**), an e-business services company, uses its portal to spread company news, exchange information, and encourage collaboration. Employees can also use corporate portals to update their human resources files and check benefits, such as their 401(k), health plans, and so on.

### Venting in Cyberspace
E-businesses can also set up a page on a corporate portal for employees to vent about the company. Postings can alert management to internal problems and provide an informal way for the company to respond without publicly airing gripes. Some external Web sites, such as the Working Wounded site (**http://www.workingwounded.com/**), already serve this function—but the downside is that posted messages can be viewed by all employees, competitors, and everyone else.

If an e-business sets up an internal cyberventing page, says Bruce Sanders, an organizational psychologist, "the key is to build the employees' sense of ownership." Arrange for an employee to sensitively edit the page (no personal attacks allowed) and promptly respond to each employee's comment. Also let employees know that the firm will do its best to respect privacy—except where postings suggest illegal or unethical actions that must be investigated. Finally, reserve this page only for employee venting; post official corporate information elsewhere.

## Trolling for Talent

As e-commerce grows, so many e-business managers are trolling for talent that recruiting has become a major headache in certain areas and specialties. Unemployment in Silicon Valley, for example, is only 1% as Web start-ups and giants compete for job applicants. In this tight labor market, companies are using a variety of recruiting techniques to attract attention. First, they post recruiting links on their home pages; second, they list jobs on e-commerce recruiting sites such as High Technology Careers (**http://www.hightechcareers.com/**); and third, they offer special incentives to attract attention.

Publicly traded e-businesses such as Amazon.com often use stock options as incentives, but smaller firms have to be even more inventive. Interwoven (**http://www.interwoven.com**), a Web content management and delivery firm, promises engineers an unusual signing bonus: a BMW Z3 roadster for two years. OnLink Technologies (**http://www.onlink.com**), which makes customer-analysis software for Web sites, promotes its monthly happy hour gatherings and "Hawaiian-shirt Fridays." To get noticed, OnLink has put its hiring message and URL on a banner towed by an airplane circling over rush hour traffic. Such techniques are likely to become more commonplace as the labor shortage continues and e-businesses battle for candidates.

## ✔ E-Business Case in Point: Softbank

Masayoshi Son's strategy for managing in the Internet age is to keep employees focused on long-term goals while encouraging immediate action. As founder and CEO of Softbank (**http://www.softbank.com**), a Tokyo-based company with stakes in Yahoo!, E*Trade, and other e-businesses, Son says: "I always start out by visualizing my final objective." His ultimate objective is to own nearly 800 e-businesses by 2004 (the company currently owns 120 e-businesses).

Son uses this vision to inspire employees and motivate quick action. For example, when Son wanted to start a new Japanese stock exchange for high-tech firms, his staff got busy and mailed out 7,000 invitations to prospective members in just one day. Supporting this vision is a policy (unusual for Japanese companies) of granting stock options to both employees and managers as tangible rewards for high performance.

Son wants his organization to evolve as the environment changes. In fact, Softbank started out as a software distributor before evolving into a leading e-commerce company. This evolution is possible because Son avoids the traditional, inflexible corporate structure and tight control over employees and companies. Instead, he encourages initiative within the organization's ranks. "I want to create an organization that self-replicates and evolves on its own," Son explains.

1. Is Masayoshi Son creating a mechanistic or an organic structure? Why?
2. Does Son seem to be a transactional or transformational leader? What are the implications for his organization?

---

# E-Business and Strategy

## Developing Strategy for E-Businesses and Legacy Businesses

The e-commerce boom is affecting many parts of the business environment, including competition, supply sources, and technology—creating new opportunities and threats for companies to consider as they develop their strategies. Book retailer Barnes & Noble, for example, responded to the growth of the Internet—and Amazon.com's success—by creating Barnesandnoble.com (**http://www.bn.com**) as a new business unit targeting consumers who prefer to buy online.

When a company starts an e-business unit, the traditional, non-Internet business unit (in this case, the book store chain) is known as the *legacy business*. In crafting its portfolio strategy, management must decide whether to integrate or separate e-businesses and legacy businesses in the portfolio. Barnes and Noble opted for separation, while software retailer Egghead opted for integration. What happened?

## Separating E-Businesses: Barnes and Noble
Barnes & Noble's portfolio strategy was to set up its Web site as a separate company (1) to avoid siphoning sales away from the stores, and (2) to avoid charging sales tax in states where the stores are located. The company differentiates its e-business by offering both lower prices and broader selection. However, with this portfolio strategy, Barnes & Noble lost an opportunity to create synergy between the two units. Because of the separation, customers can't go to the stores to return books bought on the Web site, nor can they order from the Web site when they're in the stores. So far, separation hasn't given the Web site the boost it needs to overtake Amazon.com as top online bookseller.

## Integrating E-Businesses: Egghead
The initial portfolio strategy of Egghead (**http://www.egghead.com**) was to add a Web presence without separating the e-business from the legacy business, a chain of software superstores. When the chain floundered amid competition from Web-based software outlets, Egghead changed strategy and put all its eggs in the online basket by closing the stores. After more than a year as an *e-tailer* (online retailer) of software and computer-related merchandise, Egghead merged with Onsale.com in 1999. The new Egghead.com is reaching out to consumers and small business owners with a wider product selection and both discount and auction pricing. As online competition heats up, only time—and customer response—will tell how effective Egghead's strategy will be.

## Differentiating the E-Business on the Basis of Service: Garden.com
Although many Web retailers emphasize low prices, Garden.com (**http://www.garden.com**) is one of a growing number of e-businesses that emphasize excellent service. "Live plants are an absolute nightmare to sell," admits Cliff Sharples, CEO of this leading online retailer of plants and gardening supplies. Because plants require special handling, superior customer service is an absolute requirement—and a key element of Garden.com's differentiation strategy. "We've invested heavily in customer solutions, what you usually think of as customer service," Sharples explains. "We built our own systems around the system that customer solutions representatives use when they're on the phone or answering e-mail." Garden.com's technology allows its reps to track every order, from purchase to delivery. It also allows the e-business to communicate with customers at key points in the purchase process, such as sending e-mails to confirm delivery dates.

The system also gathers and organizes customer feedback, automatically routing comments to the appropriate departments for action. "That's been enormously successful in reading what the customers want, what they like or don't like about the site," Sharples says. In addition, Garden.com often invites a customer panel to react to potential new products and services—another demonstration of its service strategy in action.

## ✔ E-Business Case in Point: Hoover's Inc.
Hoover's (**http://www.hoovers.com**) was founded in 1990 as a book publisher, targeting businesses, investors, and job seekers who wanted information about U.S. and global companies. In 1993, Hoover's forged deals to put its book content online through America Online and other services. Within six months, the firm was drawing more people online than it had ever reached offline. This realization spurred a major change in Hoover's strategy.

CEO Patrick Spain saw an opportunity to give online users access to business information—which was not, at the time, readily available electronically. Among Hoover's strengths is the ability of its 100 writers and editors to quickly gather and interpret data. An online presence would enhance this strength by allowing Hoover's to update content on 15,000 firms in 50 industries daily. Moreover, integrating a Web presence was an opportunity to directly control distribution of content, in contrast to the previous strategy of distributing books through retail channels.

Spain implemented this strategy by establishing a Web site where users could sample Hoover's content for free and then obtain more detailed information by subscription. He entered additional markets by licensing content to Microsoft's Money Central site (**http://moneycentral.msn.com**) and other sites. As this e-commerce strategy took effect, the proportion of revenues shifted from 100% books to 50% online/50% books, then 85% online/15% books. Yet the strategy didn't reduce book revenues at all. Instead, it helped Hoover's increase online revenues at a much faster pace—and with fatter gross margins.

1. Which of Porter's generic strategies does Hoover's appear to be pursuing?
2. In the Miles and Snow Typology, can Hoover's be classified as a prospector, a defender, an analyzer, or a reactor?

---

# E-Business and Finance

## Financing E-Businesses

E-businesses can quickly burn through a mountain of money as they put up Web sites, hire employees, and pay for promotions to establish their brands and attract customers. So how do entrepreneurs fund their e-businesses?

Many Internet start-ups get money from *venture capitalists (VCs)*, investment specialists who provide funding for businesses (ventures) with high, rapid growth potential. For example, eBay (**http://www.ebay.com**), the first online auction site, received its early funding from Benchmark Capital (**http://www.benchmark.com**).

Once an e-business is operating, it may raise money by going public through an *initial public offering (IPO)*, selling shares of stock to the public for the first time. Through an IPO, eBay sold 3.5 million shares in 1998 to raise $63 million for aggressive expansion. Here's a closer look at VCs and IPOs.

## Working with Venture Capitalists

Every source of funding carries a cost, including money from VCs. Although the details vary from deal to deal, VCs generally provide funding in exchange for an equity stake. If and when the e-business goes public or is acquired by another company, the VC's stake should appreciate in value. The payoff can be incredibly high. Crosspoint Venture Partners (**http://www.crosspointvc.com**) is one of a handful of VCs that have enjoyed a return on investment of 500% or more after e-businesses in which they had stakes went public.

A new twist is the *for-profit incubator*, which provides office space, business services, and management resources as well as funding, in exchange for an equity stake of as much as 50%. This set-up gives entrepreneurs more support in the early stages of business formation and growth and improves the e-business's chances of success. Idealab (**http://www.idealab.com**) is a for-profit incubator that has nurtured e-businesses such as CarsDirect (**http://www.carsdirect.com**), a car-shopping site.

## Using the Internet for IPOs

The Internet promises to bring major changes to e-business IPOs. Soon, the time-consuming blizzard of paperwork that accompanies traditional IPOs may be replaced by streamlined Web-based procedures for handling the necessary information disclosures and legal filings. Some innovators are already conducting IPO stock sales via the Web. W.R. Hambrecht, a San Francisco investment firm, has developed Open IPO, a Web-based process that allows individual investors to buy IPO stock online. Traditional IPOs attract huge purchases from a concentration of institutional investors, but the Open IPO broadens the investor base by targeting individual investors.

When Andover.Net (**http://www.andover.net/**) went IPO in late 1999, it raised more than $82 million through Open IPO. Explains Bruce Twickler, Andover's president: "Our biggest asset is Slashdot, a community site, and we needed a vehicle that would allow those community members to have access to the IPO." In fact, strong demand allowed the firm to raise its *offering price*, the price to be paid by investors who receive IPO shares just before the stock starts to trade. Instead of a $15 share price, Andover increased the offering price to $18—raising an additional $9 million from the IPO proceeds. Andover operated as a publicly traded e-business for just two months before being acquired by VA Linux in early 2000.

### ✔ E-Business Case in Point: Niku

Farzad Dibachi is a seasoned e-business entrepreneur. He sold his first e-business, Diba, to Sun Microsystems in 1997 and stayed on to work for Sun (**http://www.sun.com**) for a short time before starting Niku (**http://www.niku.com**), a multi-faceted e-business. One focus is creating Web-based software to allow consulting firms to automate their internal processes and customer billing. A second focus is iNiku.com, an online marketplace for the consulting industry. A third focus is an Internet job board. And a fourth focus is helping companies expand their internal networks—intranets—for access by partners, customers, and suppliers.

Initially, Dibachi funded Niku with some of his own money plus $60 million from private investors. Although the company still had millions in the bank by the end of 1999—available for acquisitions or operations—it had lost $29 million on 10-month sales of just $12.3 million. Facing competition from Hotjobs.com (**http://www.hotjobs.com**) and other rivals, Dibachi needed more money for growth. With Goldman Sachs as the lead investment bank, Dibachi planned an IPO to sell 8 million shares of common stock, at an offering price between $10 and $12 per share. Farzad Dibachi and his wife, both officers in the company, retained about 17% of the shares.

The deal, set for late February, was briefly postponed while Goldman Sachs hiked the offering price, one indication of the huge demand for the stock. Finally, on February 29, 2000, the stock was scheduled to begin trading with an offering price of $24—raising $192 million for Niku. At the start, the stock sold at $64 per share, and it closed its first day of trading at $69. On the second day, the price zoomed to $100, where it hovered for several days before receding. By early April, Niku's stock price had dropped to the $30s, but it revived to over $42 when the company announced plans to expand in Europe. Niku's IPO was off to a solid start.

1. How did Niku benefit when its investment bank raised the offering price?
2. Why do you think Dibachi would take Niku public instead of seeking more funding from venture capitalists?

# E-Business and Legal Studies

## Protecting Intellectual Property Online

Protecting intellectual property rights, which are among an e-business's greatest assets, can be a difficult legal challenge. Internet domain names, for example, become valuable once an e-business has successfully built its brand. This is why e-businesses worry about *cybersquatting*, the practice of claiming a domain name with the intention of reselling it at a profit. Thanks to the Trademark Cyberpiracy Prevention Act, passed in late 1999, cybersquatting is now illegal.

Patents on Internet products and processes are also valuable, providing competitive advantages and, in some cases, lucrative licensing fees. However, as e-commerce grows, the number of patent applications for Web-based processes also grows, as does the confusion over what can—and should—be protected by patent. Priceline.com and Amazon.com have been particularly aggressive in protecting their Web patents.

## Protecting Web Patents

Priceline (**http://www.priceline.com**) works hard to keep other e-businesses from infringing on its patented "name your own price" process. When Expedia.com (**http://www.expedia.com**) introduced a similar pricing technique for travel services, Priceline filed suit, charging patent infringement. The suit is still pending.

Amazon (**http://www.amazon.com**) is also highly protective of its intellectual property. It recently patented a "one click" ordering method, which allows customers to place an order with one mouse click. As soon as Amazon received this patent, it filed suit and won an injunction against Barnes and Noble (**http://www.bn.com**), which was using a similar ordering method. Barnes and Noble was forced to change to "two click" ordering.

Amazon recently received a patent for its affiliate system, which allows other Web sites to refer customers to Amazon in exchange for commissions. Barnes and Noble and many other sites use a comparable method for affiliate referrals. Could Amazon, as the patent-holder, force these e-businesses to make changes or pay licensing fees?

E-businesses and patent-law experts charge that such Web patents are overly broad, because they cover basic e-commerce methods that are hardly new or unique. "In my view, this is the single greatest threat to innovation in cyberspace," comments Harvard law professor Lawrence Lessig. To address such concerns, the U.S. Patent and Trademark Office is adding new steps to its patent review process. Meanwhile, the legal wrangling over Web patents continues.

## Protecting Privacy Online

Privacy is another hot legal issue for e-businesses. More than two-thirds of all Web sites ask their visitors for personal data so the sites can customize their offerings. Even visitors who don't volunteer data are, in many cases, being monitored by profiling firms such as DoubleClick (**http://www.doubleclick.com**). *Profiling* means tracking consumers' online activities and using the data to create an outline of each person's interests. Using *cookies* - devices that grab online user information - stored on consumers' hard drives, DoubleClick has profiled as many as 100 million Web users.

DoubleClick and other profilers allow Web users to opt out of their profiling programs. Yet privacy advocates worry that profile databases could be merged with other online data, such as postings on a newsgroup, to yield highly specific data that could threaten individual privacy. In response, Congress and the Federal Trade Commission have begun investigating privacy protection. Some states are already working on legislation to prevent e-businesses from selling personal data and to require disclosure of privacy policies.

Some e-businesses aren't waiting for legal action on privacy issues. The AltaVista search site (**http://www.altavista.com**) recently switched to an "opt-in" policy, pledging not to collect or share personal information such as name and e-mail address unless the user specifically grants permission. AltaVista is also participating in the privacy programs offered by TRUSTe (**http://www.truste.com/**), an e-business that helps Web sites develop consumer-oriented privacy policies. But is such self-regulation strong enough to protect consumer privacy online?

### ✔ E-Business Case in Point: Yet2.Com

Yet2.Com (**http://www.yet2.com**) is an e-business pioneer in exploiting the financial potential of intellectual property. Its Web site serves as a clearing-house for deals between companies that want to license patented technologies. The great-grandson of Du Pont's founder, Ben du Pont, conceived the idea while working for his family's business. Responsible for global development of Lycra, the patented Du Pont stretchy fiber, he became increasingly frustrated as he searched for new uses and licensees for the product. That's when du Pont and co-founder Chris De Bleser came up with the idea for Yet2.Com ("yet to come"), which debuted in February 2000.

Dozens of corporations have signed on to post information about their patents. Polaroid, for example, is posting data about 900 of its patents; other participants include Du Pont, Siemens, Toyota, and Boeing. Yet2.Com protects buyers by verifying that sellers actually hold the patents they are offering. Similarly, it protects sellers by checking on potential buyers before any deal proceeds.

Potential buyers can get short descriptions of available patents on the Yet2.Com site without charge. They pay $25 for a more detailed description and $1,000 for contact information about the company holding the patent. Once the buyer and seller agree on a deal, Yet2.Com receives a 10% commission, capped at a maximum of $50,000. In its first few weeks of operation, the site brokered five deals—including one involving Du Pont.

1. What does Yet2.Com do to avoid the common law tort of palming off?
2. Why would a company describe a patent on Yet2.Com without posting all the details?

---

# E-Business and Accounting

## Accounting for the New Economy

The growth in e-commerce has turned the spotlight on key issues in accounting, auditing, and taxation. When and how does an e-business recognize revenue? Does the e-business capitalize or expense costs? Should Internet sales be taxed?

The Securities and Exchange Commission (SEC) has raised questions about how these and other accounting issues affect the financial statements that investors review when deciding whether to buy an e-business's stock. It recently asked the Financial Accounting Standards Board (FASB) to examine the issues and formulate suitable guidelines for generally accepted accounting principles (GAAP).

## Accounting for Revenues
Some experts fear that pressure to make revenues look higher will tempt firms to use overly aggressive accounting techniques. This a concern because many e-businesses earn little initial profit, so investors often look at revenue growth when deciding which stock to buy.

For example, auction firms (on and off the Internet) generally charge sellers a "listing fee" when accepting items for auction as well as a transaction fee when the item is sold. Under GAAP, auction firms are expected to spread listing-fee revenues across the entire sale period; they're also expected to recognize transaction fees after the deal is complete. However, the SEC has found that some online auction sites are booking these fees right away—an accounting no-no that makes current revenues look higher.

## Accounting for Costs
Aggressive accounting treatment of costs is another concern. A few years ago, America Online (**http://www.aol.com**) spent heavily to mail out free software during a new-subscriber blitz. Saying that subscribers stay for an average of 24 months, AOL spread these marketing costs over 24 months. This controversial decision made short-term profits look good—but sharp-eyed investors questioned the practice. After deferring more than $350 million in marketing costs, AOL decided that its balance sheet would look better under a less aggressive approach, so it began recognizing these costs as incurred.

Another area where some e-businesses get aggressive is in accounting for fulfillment costs such as shipping. Non-Web businesses typically classify these under cost of sales, which affects their gross profit margins. Some e-businesses make gross profit margins look better by classifying these costs under marketing. They reason that investors will find nothing strange in using marketing to build a solid customer base, and this allows them to avoid thinning already slender profit margins. Small wonder that this accounting approach is controversial. In fact, Varsitybooks.com (**http://www.varsitybooks.com**) fired the giant KPMG as its auditor when the accounting firm objected to this approach.

## Handling Internet Sales Taxes
Should Internet sales be tax-free? The Internet Tax Freedom Act, passed in 1998, forbids the collection of special Internet taxes in the United States, but this moratorium expires in October, 2001. Meanwhile, debate rages between pro- and anti-tax factions. Many e-businesses say that without nexus—a physical presence, such as a store—they are not obligated to collect sales taxes. This position is based on a Supreme Court ruling that state and local governments cannot compel catalog and direct-mail businesses to collect sales taxes unless the firms have a physical presence in their area. These e-businesses also argue that applying sales taxes to Internet purchases will significantly slow the growth of e-commerce.

For their part, non-Internet businesses say that e-businesses should not enjoy special tax treatment. State and local governments worry about whether tax-free Internet sales would take away a sizable portion of the nearly $200 billion in sales taxes they collect annually from stores and other non-Internet businesses. And Treasury Secretary Lawrence Summers is unyielding in saying that "cyberspace should not become a tax haven that promotes evasion or avoidance of the basic taxes in our system." Expect this tax issue to simmer for months as the debate continues.

## ✔ E-Business Case in Point: Priceline.com
Should Priceline.com (**http://www.priceline.com**), which allows consumers to name their own price for airline tickets and other products, recognize revenues on a gross or a net basis? The answer hinges on whether Priceline arranges deals between seller and buyer or whether it owns the products it sells.

Travel agents typically report net revenues based on their commissions (not the full ticket price), because they are agents and do not own the tickets they sell. In contrast, when Priceline sells an airline ticket for, say, $150, it books the sale as gross revenue, even though it may have paid $100 or less for the ticket. Priceline says it briefly assumes ownership of the ticket, so it is the "merchant of record" and is exposed to all the potential risks (and rewards) of the sale. Under SEC guidelines, Priceline is therefore entitled to recognize the gross revenue. And the more gross revenue, the better the company looks.

Of course, gross revenue figures are much more impressive than net revenue figures. In one recent quarter, Priceline reported $152.2 million in gross revenues and net revenues of $18.2 million. Although Priceline's accounting procedure is legal, Jeffrey Bronchick of the money management firm Reed Conner & Birdwell observes that "it's just so gray and borderline."

1. How do you think investors would react if an e-business that reports gross revenues started reporting net revenues?
2. Should the SEC require e-businesses to report both gross and net revenues? Why?

---

# E-Business and Economics

## Understanding the New Economy

What is the new economy? Also called the *Internet economy*, the *new economy* is comprised of businesses that generate all or some of their revenues from the Internet or related goods and services. The Center for Research on Electronic Commerce divides the new economy into four layers. (1) The Internet infrastructure is made up of companies that make hardware, software, and connections for the electronic network. (2) Internet applications are covered by companies that provide software, training, and other applications for facilitating e-commerce. (3) Internet intermediaries are companies that act as brokers and agents to bring buyers and sellers together online. And (4) Internet commerce consists of companies that sell directly to customers online.

Clearly, the new economy covers a lot more than *e-tailers* (Internet retailers) such as eToys (**http://www.etoys.com**), which are part of the fourth layer. The first layer includes Internet service providers (ISPs) such as Mindspring (**http://www.mindspring.com**) as well as server manufacturers such as Dell (**http://www.dell.com**). The second layer includes search software makers such as Inktomi (**http://www.inktomi.com**) and multimedia software developers such as RealNetworks (**http://www.realnetworks.com**). And the third layer includes online travel agents such as Expedia.com (**http://www.expedia.com**) and online brokerage firms such as E*Trade (**http://www.etrade.com**).

In the old (pre-Internet) economy, buying and selling occurred in the marketplace, a physical location such as a town square or, more recently, a shopping mall. In the new economy, buyers and sellers interact electronically in a *marketspace*, an electronic marketplace. Increasingly, both consumers and businesses are completing marketspace exchanges without cash.

## Moving Toward A Cashless Society

The popularity of credit and debit cards has long fueled speculation about movement toward a *cashless society* in which plastic takes the place of currency. Now e-commerce is opening the door to additional cashless alternatives such as electronic cash and electronic barter.

*Electronic cash (e-cash)*, an electronic cash substitute, is an appealing alternative to credit cards for several reasons. First, not everyone has a credit card, especially outside the United States. Second, some Web surfers are too young to qualify for credit. Third, some consumers want anonymity when buying online. And fourth, some consumer transactions are too small to be profitably settled by credit card. Trivnet (**http://www.trivnet.com**) and iPIN (**http://www.ipin.com**) are two sites that operate e-cash systems. Once consumers sign up with Trivnet or iPIN, they can buy from participating Web sites by clicking on a special payment link and entering a password. All purchases are added to the consumer's ISP bill or telephone bill.

*Electronic barter (e-barter)*, a high-tech twist on the ancient system of barter, is already replacing some cash transactions among consumers and businesses. "Barter could change the face of global e-commerce," notes Professor Mohan Sawhney of Northwestern University's Kellogg School. Through online intermediaries such as BarterTrust.com (**http://www.bartertrust.com**), businesses anywhere in the world can efficiently exchange goods or services without any cash changing hands. Sites such as WebSwap (**http://www.webswap.com**) allow consumers to barter video games and other items. E-barter is poised to capture a larger portion of the global barter market, in which more than $14 billion worth of goods and services are exchanged every year.

## Operating in the B2B Marketspace

*B2B (business-to-business) online markets*—Web sites that facilitate the exchange of goods and services among organizational buyers and sellers—are among today's hottest marketspaces. These B2B marketspaces aim to reduce business-buying costs, expand access to more suppliers, and slash the time and paperwork needed to complete purchases.

Some B2B online markets, also known as B2B online exchanges, are operated by third parties that bring together buyers and sellers in a particular industry or product category. For example, ChemConnect (**http://ww.chemconnect.com**) facilitates the buying and selling of chemicals and plastics. Other B2B online markets are operated by groups of industry participants. For example, GlobalNetXChange (**http://www.globalnetxchange.com/**), founded by Sears and Carrefour (quickly joined by Kroger's and other major retailers), serves the buying needs of retailers worldwide.

### ✔ E-Business Case in Point: The B2B Auto-Parts Market

General Motors, Ford, and DaimlerChrysler are teaming up to launch an independent B2B online auto-parts market that could become the largest e-business of all time. Combined, the three companies spend nearly $250 billion on auto parts and supplies every year. The site—debuting soon—replaces each automaker's separate procurement site and will be open to other automakers, as well. When fully operational, the site will link some 30,000 suppliers and lead to significant buying efficiencies. GM, for example, believes the site will yield yearly savings of $500 million.

However, the Federal Trade Commission is concerned that the site may discourage competition by controlling auto-parts prices. It also worries that such industry-consortium B2B online markets could become potential monopolies because of their high volume and broad reach. All B2B online markets will be watching how the FTC handles the auto-parts market site.

1. If the U.S. automobile industry is an oligopoly, how could a B2B online auto-parts market founded by the three automakers evolve into a monopoly?
2. Is this B2B auto-parts market part of the input market or the output market? How do you know?

# E-Business and Business Communication

## Writing for Internet Audiences

How can business communicators reach those fast-clicking online readers? Just encouraging readers to give a Web page more than a glance, let alone motivating them to read to the end, can be a challenge. Experienced Internet writers suggest opening with a brief, informative preview of the site's material. This preview will give readers a reason to continue scrolling through.

Even when readers plunge in, they may not keep reading if online sections seem too long or disjointed. That's why experts recommend organizing the material into concise, manageable sections with headings that clearly signal content. Still, readers of online material do not always start at the beginning, nor do they necessarily read to the end. As a result, Internet writers need to provide contextual clues within each section to keep readers on track and to clarify the links between ideas. Knowing that readers may skip around, writers should also touch on key ideas in more than one section.

To make a personal connection with online readers, use *you* and *yours* often and use a less formal tone (where appropriate). Also, experts stress the importance of polishing and proofreading every Internet document—more than once. There's no telling how long some messages will be posted on the Web, so sloppy or inaccurate writing could be on public view for months or even years.

## Steering Clear of Spam

From the sender's perspective, one of the Internet's strengths as a communication medium is the ability to send messages quickly and fairly inexpensively to anyone anywhere. Yet from the receiver's perspective, this strength has led to annoyances such as *spam*, unsolicited e-mail messages (also known as *junk e-mail*). Spam of all sorts—from bulk e-mailings of fraudulent offers to legitimate notices of online sales—can quickly fill up online mailboxes and strain network capacity.

Fourteen states now regulate the use of spam. Some states, such as Colorado, require that unsolicited e-mail carry a subject line such as "ADV" plus a brief description of the offer. Some states require that messages explain how to *opt out*—request to be removed from the subscriber list. In addition, at least six anti-spam laws have been proposed at the federal level. To avoid being labeled a *spammer*, IBM (**http://www.ibm.com**) and many other companies are taking the audience-friendly approach of inviting people to *opt in*—sign up to receive messages. This strategy increases the chances that receivers will open the e-mail messages rather than deleting them unread.

## Keeping E-Mail in Compliance

Many brokerage firms welcome customer contact by phone and by mail—but not by e-mail. Why? To prevent misleading statements, the content of e-mail messages discussing securities are subject to strict government regulations (as are securities advertisements and other written messages). The rules also require brokerage firms to store e-mail messages for three years, in case the Securities and Exchange Commission or another government agency wants a look. Given the lengthy storage period and the tight rules on wording, e-mail is simply too much trouble for many brokerages.

Those brokerage firms that do use e-mail must screen outgoing messages to ensure compliance with the regulations—adding more complications. "You have to search for inappropriate activity," says Jim Morris, compliance officer at the brokerage firm Edward Jones (**http://www.edwardjones.com**). "You have to have systems in place to prove you do the search. And you have to have systems in place to prove you have the systems in place." Now some brokerage firms, including PaineWebber (**http://www.painewebber.com**), are testing the use of software that automatically checks brokers' e-mail messages for questionable phrases such as "hot tip." Supervisors can then follow up by reading questionable messages found by the software and discussing changes with the brokers involved.

## ✔ E-Business Case in Point: IBM

So many audiences, so many messages. That's the challenge IBM faced in using the Internet to communicate with investors, job seekers, small business customers, software developers, home and home-office PC users, and business partners. IBM's solution was to create a mini-site for each audience, all connected to the main IBM Web site. The wording and offerings on these mini-sites are carefully tailored for each audience's specific needs. So when a particular product or service is discussed on multiple mini-sites, the messages stress different features, benefits, and uses for different audiences.

In addition, IBM offers free subscriptions to several e-mail newsletters that cover new product announcements, usage tips, and special promotions. Visitors to the IBM mini-sites can opt in to receive any or all of these newsletters. They can also customize content by selecting areas of interest and even specify when newsletters should be delivered. Business partners—firms that sell to or buy from IBM—can even customize the data that IBM's Web pages display when they log on. Paying close attention to the information its audiences want, and when they want it, has helped IBM build goodwill and a positive image in cyberspace.

1. Why would IBM continue to send e-mail newsletters to people who do not buy the company's products?
2. How does IBM apply the "you" attitude to its Internet communications?

---

# E-Business and MIS

## Supporting E-Commerce Operations

Behind the scenes, organizations are using two types of private networks to support their online operations—intranets and extranets. An *intranet*—an internal computer network based on Internet technology—facilitates communication throughout the organization. Some intranets handle functional applications such as human resource management, while other intranets have broader applications. For example, the intranet at Scripps Health (**http://www.scrippshealth.org**), a nonprofit hospital group, gives its 2,600 doctors instant access to policy manuals, care instructions, medical journals, and other information.

An *extranet* is a private network that the organization makes available to authorized users outside the organization, such as suppliers and distributors. For example, the New York Stock Exchange (**http://www.nyse.com**) extranet allows member brokers to transmit buy and sell orders quickly, securely, and inexpensively.

Extranets can be targeted to narrow user groups, as well. Shell, the global oil company, created a special extranet as a central source for the company's official brand images, standards, and guidelines. This extranet, which replaced costly printed brand manuals, is open only to Shell marketing specialists and advertising agencies around the world. Extranets and intranets are becoming more commonplace as organizations seek paperless operations and as the e-commerce marketplace expands.

## Using Application Service Providers (ASPs)

The headaches of managing application software may become distant memories as Internet-delivered software solutions grow in popularity. Now businesses can eliminate the hassles of developing and updating specialized application software by going through an *application service provider (ASP)*, a business that rents application software via the Internet (or via telecommunications networks) in exchange for usage or monthly fees. Because ASPs are responsible for software development, maintenance, and upgrades, users need not invest heavily in their own staff and equipment to create, debug, and update their application software programs.

ASPs are just being launched, yet demand is already so strong that they could account for half of all software sales by 2003. This diverse market pits smaller, specialized ASPs against established software firms such as Oracle (**http://www.oracle.com**). Telecommunications giants, including AT&T (**http://www.att.com/**), are also entering the fray, creating partnerships with a number of ASP partners in order to offer small and medium-sized businesses a range of application software packages. As a result of the proliferation of ASPs and the availability of many outsourcing suppliers, business customers seeking alternatives to in-house systems management have more choices than ever.

## Enhancing Online Customer Service

Despite the increasing popularity of online shopping, up to 80% of all the online transactions that customers start do not get completed. Now an offshoot of *Internet telephony*—the transmission of telephone voice conversations via the Internet—is helping e-businesses improve the transaction-completion rate by providing immediate online customer service support. Here's how live online voice technology works: When a Web customer clicks a special service button or icon, the customer can ask questions or get product details through an instant voice conversation with a customer service representative. Customers with computers containing a microphone and speakers can talk with representatives without picking up a telephone. Customers whose computers are not properly equipped generally have the option of receiving a phone call or using text chat for conversations.

A variety of e-businesses are using this voice technology. Camera e-tailer Camera World (**http://www.cameraworld.com**) found through testing that it completed more sales when customers were able to talk with representatives using the live online voice technology it rents from Web telephony ASP eFusion (**http://www.efusion.com**). McAfee Software (**http://www.mcafeehelp.com**) allows customers with questions about the firm's software to talk with technical specialists using voice technology rented from an ASP called EchoPass (**http://www.echopass.com**). As the quality of Internet voice transmissions improves, e-businesses will find even more applications for this technology in the coming years.

### ✔ E-Business Case in Point: Capitol

Capitol (**http://www.capitol.fr**), a start-up online brokerage firm based in Paris, is using Internet telephony customer service to attract customers in the increasingly crowded European brokerage services market. Dominique Velter, Capitol's president, knows that many of her customers are new both to the Internet and to stock investments. These customers often need detailed guidance working their way through the portfolio management and product offerings on Capitol's site. However, customers may hesitate to call the broker because phone calls are costly in Europe. That's where Capitol's online voice customer service comes in to play.

Once customers log onto the Capitol site, they can click on a service icon to talk with a representative at any time, without adding phone charges. Although voice conversations with reps humanize the Web site's service, when some people first hear a representative's voice, "it takes them a moment to collect themselves and speak to the computer," says a Capitol employee. But apparently people do adjust. Thanks to Internet telephony, Capitol is on track to sign twice as many new customers as it originally expected this year.

1. Is the software that powers this Internet telephony considered application or system software?
2. What concerns might customers have about receiving customer service assistance via Internet telephony?

---

# E-Business and Decision Science

## Managing Links Online in the Supply Chain

Given the complex flows of materials, services, and information among all the links in the supply chain, it's not surprising that many businesses find supply-chain management a major challenge. Now businesses are harnessing ever more sophisticated technology—including the Internet—to better manage inputs, outputs, and supply chain links.

*Enterprise resource planning (ERP)* systems go beyond manufacturing resource planning (MRP II) systems to allow more comprehensive planning and control of operations. ERP systems allow firms to manage different levels of materials, services, and data traveling through the entire supply chain, from suppliers to production facilities to distribution partners and to customers. Supplementing ERP systems, other tools for managing the supply chain are e-procurement, online catalogues, online requests for quotes (RFQs), and advanced planning and scheduling systems.

## Moving Purchasing to the Web

Traditionally, procurement required piles of paperwork and lengthy approval procedures. At IBM (**http://www.ibm.com**), for example, employees had to wait more than 30 days for official approvals to buy even small items such as pens. Now *e-procurement*, purchasing via the Internet, is streamlining the procurement process, slashing the cost and the time needed to place an order. When IBM employees submit purchase requests through the company's Web-based e-procurement system, they can get approvals in less than two hours.

Some e-procurement systems are built around an *online catalogue*, a Web-based presentation of product information similar to a printed catalogue. Beer marketer Adolph Coors (**http://www.coors.com**), for instance, used to send distributors and restaurants a printed catalogue of Coors brand merchandise such as belt buckles. But juggling products from 72 suppliers and orders from nearly 700 distributors proved so difficult that Coors switched to an online catalogue. Now when distributors order from the online catalog, the system automatically arranges for delivery while transmitting sales information to suppliers for reorders.

Even RFQs are moving to the Internet, thanks to sites such as BizBuyer (**http://www.bizbuyer.com**) and SupplierMarket.com (**http://www.suppliermarket.com**). In the past, a buyer would prepare purchase specifications and then mail or fax the information to suppliers, asking for price quotes. Responses could take days. Today, companies such as Simmons, the mattress manufacturer, are finding new suppliers—and shaving their costs—by posting RFQs on special Web sites. These sites invite companies to post their purchasing needs so suppliers can respond. Using SupplierMarket.com saved Simmons $400,000 on a single purchase. "It's a neat way to get your requirements out there in front of a lot of suppliers quickly and efficiently," comments the vice-president of materials management.

## Improving Planning and Scheduling

Making decisions about output is another aspect of supply-chain management. Today many businesses can use an *advanced planning and scheduling (APS) system*, a computerized system that helps businesses evaluate varying input levels to plan for optimum production efficiency. A business using an APS system (often as a part of an ERP system) can quickly see how different combinations of resources such as materials and plant capacity will affect production. The result: lower safety stock, fewer bottlenecks that slow production, and more realistic order delivery dates. Fern-

Howard, a U.K. manufacturer of energy-efficient lighting products, reduced its inventory levels by 15% after installing an ASP system.

Many ASP systems run on the Internet, allowing personnel at different plants to collaborate on planning and scheduling. In addition, more businesses are giving suppliers access to their ASP systems. When suppliers can see their customers' production schedules, they can more accurately forecast demand and deliver supplies as needed. The result is improved efficiency—and lower costs—throughout the supply chain.

### ✔ E-Business Case in Point: Eaton

Nearly a century old, Eaton Corporation (**http://www.eaton.com**) is learning new Web-based operations management tricks. Eaton, a maker of engine parts, hydraulics, and electronics, had no e-commerce strategy before acquiring Aeroquip-Vickers, a maker of engine hoses and fittings. Then Eaton's CEO saw Aeroquip's Web site, an online catalogue that allows distributors to check Aeroquip's inventory levels, transmit orders, and track fulfillment.

Eaton's management quickly recognized the competitive benefit: Although rivals post inventory levels online, their information is not always up-to-the-minute. Aeroquip, however, constantly updates its inventory levels, so distributors can tell which items are in stock and ready to ship. Seizing this opportunity to speed orders and slash ordering costs, Eaton expanded Aeroquip's e-commerce strategy to all its divisions.

Distributors like the system. "It's so user-friendly," comments one distributor. "When a customer calls me to buy a part that both Aeroquip and a competitor sell, rather than having customers wait one or two days before I find out if a competitor has the product, I can put them on hold, check Aeroquip's inventory online, come back with an immediate answer, and often take their order right there." Four months after plunging into e-commerce, Eaton was already ringing up millions of dollars in online sales and on track to shave $2 million from operations costs during the first year alone.

1. What effect is Eaton's e-commerce strategy likely to have on the inventory levels of its distributors?
2. Should Aeroquip let its distributors and suppliers view inventory levels of raw materials and work-in-process as well as finished goods?

# Chapter 2
# Searching the Internet

The Internet contains plenty of valuable information, but it's not always easy to find what you want—unless you have a good search strategy, based on an open text search or a subject tree search.

In an *open text search*, the search engine scans the Web looking for a word or group of words you have entered as your search string. The search engine then lists links to Web pages it determines are most relevant to your keyword(s). AltaVista (**http://www.altavista.com**) and Google (**http://www.google.com**) are two of the many open text search engines you can use.

Subject tree searches take a different approach. A *subject tree* is a catalog of a great number of pages on the Web, neatly organized by category, sub-category, sub-sub-category, and so on. Yahoo! (**http://www.yahoo.com**) is one of the most comprehensive subject tree indexes; Snap (**http://www.snap.com**) and LookSmart (**http://www.looksmart.com**) are other well-known subject tree sites. How do subject tree and open text searches work?

## Subject Tree Search

Suppose you want to know more about mutual funds. To conduct a subject tree search, point your browser to the Snap home page (**http://www.snap.com**). You'll see a number of categories and, below each, several subcategories.

Mutual funds is most closely related to "Finance," so click on that category. The bottom of the next screen shows additional subcategories. "Investing" is the subcategory most closely related to mutual funds, so click on it. Now you'll see a new subcategory listing—with "Mutual Funds" as one of your choices. On the "Mutual Funds" page, you can explore "Fund Families" or "Mutual Fund Guides" or any other link of interest. You can also go directly to any of the Web sites listed below the subcategories. See Figure 2.1.

Here's the path you followed to reach the mutual funds subcategory:

Finance ⇨ Investing ⇨ Mutual Funds

There is a bit more work involved in a subject tree search than in an open text search, but the results are often worth the effort. Remember, people — not robot programs — compile subject trees, and these people cut out links that are useless. Also, subject trees can help orient your search by showing you sites that fall into the same category. This grouping may lead you to discover sites you might not have found using an open text search.

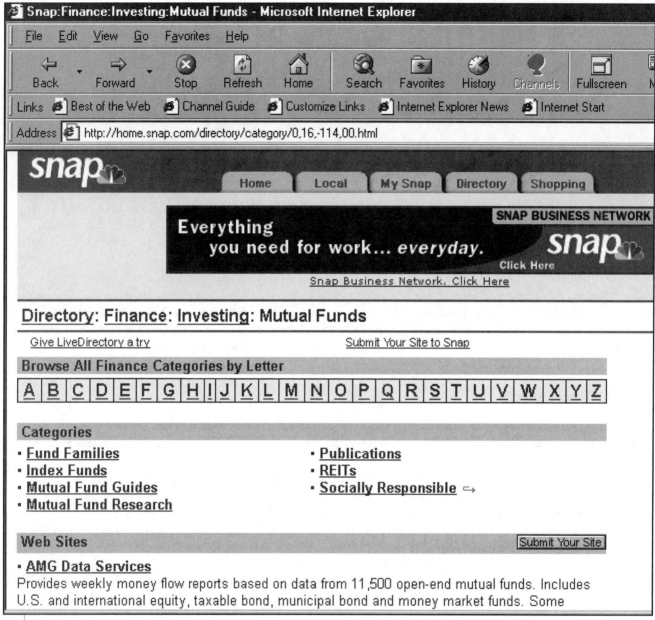

Figure 2.1. Snap is a subject tree index that helps searchers find information by drilling down through an organized hierarchy of subcategories.

## Open Text Search

In an open text search, you enter a keyword for the search engine to use in scouring the Web. The search engine returns a listing of all the Web pages that match your keyword, ranked in order of relevance. Generally, pages on which the keyword appears the greatest number of times receive a higher relevance rating. (Be aware that a few search engines display some sites higher in the result listing in exchange for payment from those sites.) Since thousands of pages can contain the same keyword, it is important for you to be as specific as possible when you conduct an open text search.

Suppose you want to locate information about the Nike company using the open search feature of Google (http://www.google.com). Enter the word Nike in the search box and press the "Enter" key on your keyboard or the "Google Search" button. (On Google, pressing the "I'm Feeling Lucky" button takes you directly to the first Web page listed in the search results.)

Google displays its "Google Search" results in two ways. First, it lists the relevant categories (from the subject tree index portion of the site). Then it provides a listing of sites that contain the keyword, with the most relevant site at the top of the listing. The first 10 matches are displayed on the first page, unless you use the box at the top of the screen to request 30 or 100 matches per page. Press the "Next" button at the bottom of the screen to view the next set of Web sites that contain the keyword. Note that Google uses indentation to show which pages are connected to a particular Web site. See Figure 2.2

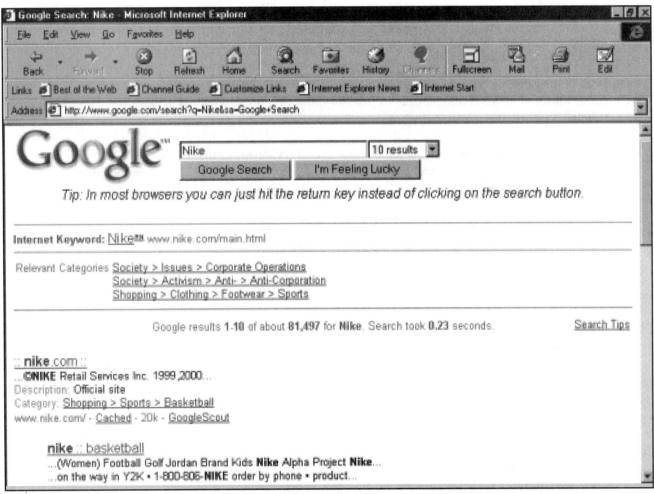

Figure 2.2. During a keyword search, Google displays a directory of topics plus links to specific Web sites.

## Your Turn
Using Snap (**http://www.snap.com**), locate the site for *Advertising Age* magazine, beginning at the top level of the directory and drilling down until you find a direct link. Now use the keyword "Advertising Age" on Google (**http://www.google.com**) to locate the same site.

| Keywords | Number of Snap categories | Number of Google matches |
|---|---|---|
| Advertising Age | | |

On Snap, how many levels of categories did you move through to reach the *Advertising Age* site? How many matches did Google turn up for the same keywords? Where in the listing of results for each search engine did the *Advertising Age* Web site appear?

## Advanced Search Techniques
Sometimes a simple search turns up rather strange results or a huge number of Web sites, as in your Google search. Using advanced search techniques allows you to conduct a more specific open text search and receive more relevant results.

Some of these search techniques are based on the way search engines determine the relevance of a Web page. AltaVista, like many search engines, aims to position the most relevant documents at the top of the list, based on the following criteria:

- the keywords are found in the first few words of the document
- the keywords are found close to one another in the document
- the document contains more than one instance of the keywords

Advanced search techniques include the use of pluses, minuses, quotation marks, and wildcards.

### Pluses and Minuses
During an open text search, you can use plus and minus signs to specify what you want a search engine to include and exclude. On the AltaVista search engine (**http://www.altavista.com**), a plus means that you want the word to appear on a Web page; a minus means that you don't want it to appear. So +inflation -currency gives you all sites containing the word "inflation" but not "currency." Conversely, -inflation +currency gives you all sites without "inflation" but with "currency."

### Your Turn
Go to the AltaVista site (**http://www.altavista.com**) and try the inflation and currency searches. Be sure to include a space between the words, or AltaVista will think you are searching for one long word.

| You Type | It Means |
|---|---|
| +inflation -currency | Find all pages that have information on inflation but not currency. |

About how many documents were returned by this first query?

| You Type | It Means |
|---|---|
| -inflation +currency | Find all pages that do not cover inflation but have information on currency. |

About how many documents were returned by this second query?

## Keep it in Quotes

When you want the search words to appear right next to each other with no words in between, type your keywords in quotes. Use AltaVista for the following two searches.

| You Type | It Means |
|---|---|
| current economic forecast | Find all sites that have the words "current," "economic," and "forecast" (not necessarily right next to each other, not necessarily in that order). |

About how many Web pages did this query find?

Now use quotation marks to find sites where all three words appear right next to each other.

| You Type | It Means |
|---|---|
| "current economic forecast" | Find all sites that have the words "current" and "economic" and "forecast" appearing right next to each other, in that order. |

About how many Web pages did the query find?

Now combine a plus symbol and quotation marks to find just those sites that mention Asia's current economic forecast.

| You Type | It Means |
|---|---|
| +"current economic forecast" +asia | Find all sites that have the words "current economic forecast" appearing right next to each other. Those same pages must also contain the word "asia." |

About how many Web pages did this query find? As these searches indicate, narrowing a search using quotation marks works best when you want to find a string of three words or more. Sometimes searches for two words reveal the same results with or without using quotes.

## When in Doubt, Use Lowercase
You may have noticed that in all of the examples above, the keywords were typed in lowercase letters, even when searching for a proper name, such as Asia. The reason for this is that lowercase keywords match both lower and uppercase, but uppercase matches uppercase only. So, if some Webmaster forgets to capitalize Asia, you'll still find that site.

## A Star for the Wildcard
What if you are looking for information on European free trade zones? It is reasonable to assume that a search for Europe free trade zones might also produce good results. Rather than run two searches — European free trade zones and Europe free trade zones — you can use the wildcard notation to match all words that start with Europe (that is, both Europe and European) by typing europe*. The keywords you enter would therefore be +europe* +"free trade zones" for this open text search.

## More about Advanced Search Techniques
Most search sites tell users how to conduct advanced searches. For example, you can read AltaVista's Advanced Search Tutorial (**http://doc.altavista.com/adv_search/ast_i_index.shtml**) to learn more about different search engines and the use of symbols and words to narrow your search. Another good starting point is the Search Engines link on About the Web (**http://www.about-the-web.com/**).

You can get more detailed information about various search engines and search strategies on the Search Engine site (**http://searchenginewatch.com/**). Look for ideas on how and where to search by browsing the links on the 4Anything site (**http://4search.4anything.com/**). And you'll find links to search tutorials, search engines, and specialized search strategies on the Search IQ site (**http://www.searchiq.com/guide/**).

## Go Beyond with Metasearch

Each search engine uses its own technique or strategy to conduct a search. That's why entering the same keyword on two search engines will usually turn up different results. Want a more comprehensive search? Try a metasearch site, such as Dogpile (**http://www.dogpile.com**), MetaCrawler (**http://www.metacrawler.com**), or Ixquick (**http://www.ixquick.com**).

Metasearch sites send your keyword out to a number of search engines at one time. Within seconds, you get back a listing of results from all the search engines that found sites containing your keyword. This saves you the time and trouble of entering your keyword in one search engine after another.

The number of search engines covered varies by metasearch site. Dogpile works through 18 search engines, including Google, Yahoo, LookSmart, and AltaVista. Ixquick works through 14 search engines, including HotBot, Fast Search, and Snap. MetaCrawler works through 12 search engines, including Excite, WebCrawler, and Lycos (see Figure 2.3). All of these metasearch sites allow you to specify which search engines you want to use. Dogpile even lets you indicate the order in which you want the search engines contacted.

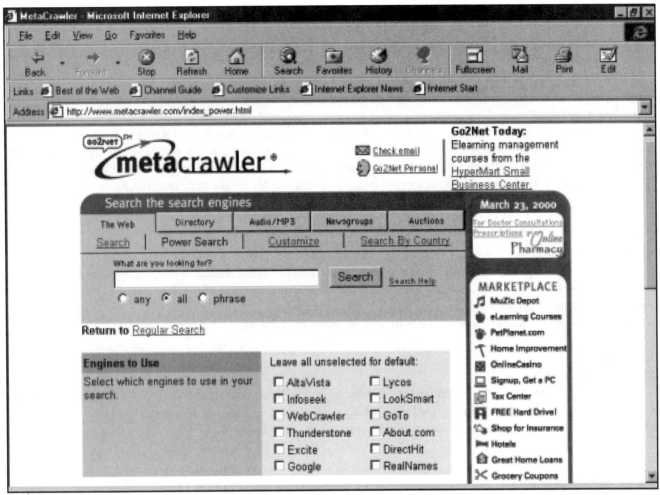

Figure 2.3. Narrowing your search on the Metacrawler Power Search site.

## Your Turn

Compare the results of two searches using the same keywords on different metasearch sites. First go to Dogpile (**http://www.dogpile.com**) and then go to MetaCrawler (**http://www.metacrawler.com**) to search for information on "global business."

| Keywords | Number of Dogpile matches | Number of MetaCrawler matches |
|---|---|---|
| "global business" | | |

Which site turns up more matches? How are the results displayed on each metasearch site? How relevant are most of the matches returned on each site?

# More Search Engines

This chapter showed you how to use Snap, Google, AltaVista, Dogpile, and MetaCrawler. Here are some more good search engines to try.

### About.com
### http://www.about.com
At About.com (formerly known as MiningCo.com), people – called guides –search out information and sites, then post the details on About.com's pages according to category. Type in a keyword and About.com will suggest numerous sites, each recommended by guides who are specialists in their fields and each containing additional links in that area of interest. You can e-mail these guides for more information, too. Guides update their category pages weekly – sometimes daily – and they also host live chats and forum discussions, publish newsletters, and recommend books.

### Excite
### http://www.excite.com
Excite searches the entire Web not only for your keywords but also for related topics. If you find an interesting site among those listed in your search results, you can click on "Search for more documents like this one" to find related pages. During a search, you can add another search word to your keyword with one click. Excite can conduct searches in eleven languages, a valuable feature if you want to find international data.

### GoTo.com
### http://www.goto.com
GoTo.com is a basic search engine, developed in response to feature-heavy engines such as Lycos and Yahoo! Its motto is "Search Made Simple." GoTo offers some broad subject categories as well as open text search capabilities. It also offers the option of screening out adult-oriented sites when results are displayed.

### HotBot
### http://www.hotbot.com
HotBot allows you to specify the Web page publication dates, the media content (pictures, video, audio), and other criteria to make your search results more specific. Another nice feature: Once you get the first listing of results, you can conduct additional searches within that listing.

### Ixquick
### http://www.ixquick.com
This metasearch site is fast and displays only the most relevant results, listed according to how they are ranked by the various search engines. Because different search engines rank sites according to different criteria, a site that receives high rankings by multiple engines is likely to contain valuable information. In addition, Ixquick eliminates duplicates, so a site appears only once in the listing of results.

### Lycos
### http://www.lycos.com
Lycos organizes Internet sites into categories, which Lycos' editors continually update and expand. Lycos has a powerful search capability, as well. When you conduct a search, the first set of results consists of Web sites that are ranked according to popularity; the second set consists of other Web sites that not ranked by popularity; and the third set consists of news articles from Internet news sources.

## Magellan
http://magellan.excite.com

Magellan is programmed to look for documents containing your exact search words as well as for ideas linked to those words. Then Magellan lists 10 search results at a time in decreasing relevance order. Each result lists its relevance percentage -- 100% being the most relevant – to your search word(s). If you find a good site, click on the "Find Similar" link, which will take you to sites similar to the one you thought was helpful.

## MSN Web Search
http://search.msn.com

This Microsoft search site allows you to specify the type of content (images, audio, special effects) to be found on a site. It also has the ability to search only sites from particular regions or only sites in specific languages. The site displays 10, 15, 20, 50, or 100 results at a time, and allows you to save your results if your browser is Internet Explorer (Version 5.0 or higher).

## Yahoo!
http://www.yahoo.com

The Yahoo! subject tree directory was started in 1994 by David Filo and Jerry Yang, Ph.D., as a way to keep track of their personal interests on the Internet. Today, Yahoo! is one of the most popular online search sites. When you enter keywords, Yahoo! will automatically return categories and sites that contain all of those words. You can easily customize your search, and searches on this site are not case-sensitive (that is, it doesn't matter whether words are uppercase or lower-case). Throughout Yahoo! categories are shown in bold text and end-sites are listed in plain text. Look for the latest site additions under "What's New."

# Evaluating and Using Search Results

Just because information is on the Internet doesn't mean that it's complete, accurate, or objective. Some sites, such as the Dow Jones Business Directory (**http://www.bd.dowjones.com/index.asp**), rate other sites on the basis of content, speed, navigation, and design. These ratings can help you identify the most valuable sites. But how can you evaluate other sources of information you uncover during an Internet search?

## Determining the Credibility of Internet Sources
Before you use data from any online source, ask:

- *What do you know about the source?* When in doubt, seek out online sources that have a reputation for reliability. Many Web sites are sponsored by well-known organizations, such as major newspapers, that have earned a reputation for integrity. However, some Web sites don't even identify their sponsors. So be wary if the source is completely unfamiliar or has a questionable reputation.

- *Does the source seem biased?* Think about whether the source is likely to have a definite point of view on certain issues. For example, when you browse the Web site of the American Association of Retired Persons, bear in mind that the information is likely to reflect that group's role as an advocate for people over 50 years old. Knowing the organization's purpose and viewpoint can help you interpret any information you use from that source.

- *What is the original source of the information?* In many cases, Web sites and databases draw their information from other sources, such as government studies. If the original source is noted, take time to evaluate its reputation and potential for bias before you use the data. If no original source is indicated, approach the data with caution.

- *Can you verify the source's information?* Before you use information from an online source, try to find another source to verify the data. You can use another search engine to scan the Internet for the same kind of data provided by at least one other reliable source. The ability to confirm information serves as a valuable check on the data's accuracy—and the accuracy of its source.

- *Does the source's information seem reasonable to you?* As a final check on any online source, use your judgment to evaluate the data and the conclusions. Given the other facts you have uncovered on the subject, does this source's information seem unreasonable or out of line? If so, look further for a more credible source.

## How Does Plagiarism Apply to Internet Sources?

Online research is so convenient that you may be tempted simply to copy material from an Internet source and paste it intact within your document. However, unless your sources are properly documented, you will be plagiarizing. Whether you're working on a term paper or researching a business report, you should cite your source when you (1) quote word-for-word, (2) closely paraphrase, or (3) repeat a series of phrases from documents posted on the Internet. This includes news articles, books or excerpts, surveys, speeches, transcripts of online discussions, manuals, and any material on Web pages sponsored by individuals, corporations, schools, nonprofit groups, or government agencies. When in doubt, you can avoid even the hint of plagiarism by fully documenting your sources.

# Chapter 3
# Career Development on the Internet

On the Internet, career development is just a mouse-click away. You may already be familiar with traditional job-search resources such as the *Occupational Outlook Handbook* (for identifying high-growth occupations), *What Color Is Your Parachute?* (for practical tips on how to get a job), and the help-wanted ads in your local newspaper. Now the Internet has many of the same resources online and ready for instant access—along with an ever-expanding variety of additional job-related Web sites.

Whether you're looking for a new job or want to explore an entirely new occupation, you can gather a great deal of information without leaving your keyboard. By launching your Web browser and moving onto the Internet, you will be able to search for career opportunities, find job openings in your chosen field, investigate potential employers, exchange ideas with other job seekers, and enlarge your circle of contacts.

Remember that changes on the Internet occur almost daily, so you are bound to find something new or different every time you log on. From career counseling centers to job-search newsgroups, virtual job fairs to commercial résumé databanks, more and more Internet options are becoming available to help bring employers and potential employees together.

This constant change also means that your favorite Web site may have new features or even a new location next time you go online. As a result, don't be surprised to find a slightly different look or perhaps a new address for the sites mentioned in this chapter.

## How to Research Careers and Employers

A good way to start your online job search is by researching various occupations and industries that sound appealing. This way, you can identify career paths that match your interests, see which have strong potential for future growth, and then focus your search accordingly.

To learn more about specific occupations, bookmark the latest edition of the *Occupational Outlook Handbook*, from the U.S. Department of Labor. This multi-faceted site describes a wide range of occupations, detailing each job's duties, training requirements, employment trends, and future prospects (**http://stats.bls.gov/ocohome.htm**). For the latest news about employment projections, earnings, and the effect of regional economic conditions, check the news releases posted online by the U.S. Bureau of Labor Statistics (**http://stats.bls.gov/newsrels.htm**).

Many state employment offices maintain Web sites bursting with comprehensive information about occupations, industries, wages, and many other topics. You can locate your state's job service site by launching Excite or another search tool and searching for "state employment service" or a similar phrase. Once you find your state's site, be sure to explore each hyperlink—you never know where these connections will lead you.

For example, the Career Resource Library on the New York State Department of Labor Web site (**http://www.labor.state.ny.us/html/library.htm**) contains a wealth of hyperlinks to state and regional employment trends and projections; national, statewide, and local wage rates; industry descriptions; and hyperlinks to dozens of other sites with tips on vital subjects such as résumé preparation, training and education, job applications, and interviewing (see Figure 3.1). Even job seekers outside New York will be interested in the general guidance available on this site.

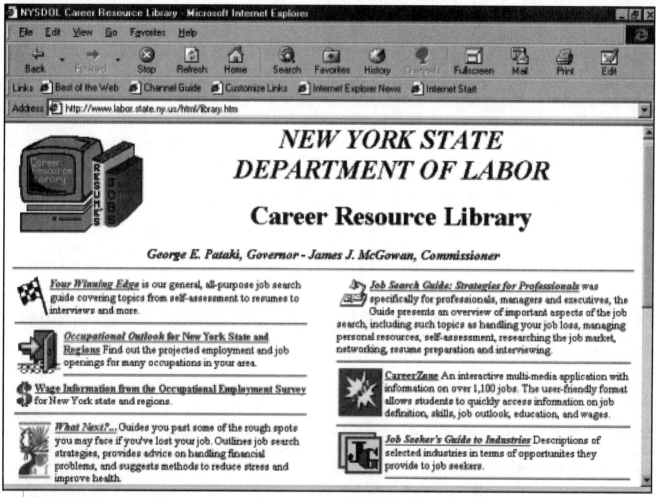

Figure 3.1. Check out the Career Resource Library at the Web site of the New York State Department of Labor.

Be sure to find out about your school's career services, which are often available online through the campus placement office. In addition, you may want to browse other university career counseling Web sites for more information about various occupations. Here are just two samples: The "Career Exploration Links" maintained by the University of California at Berkeley (**http://www.uhs.berkeley.edu/CareerLibrary/links/careerme.htm**) and the "Exploring Occupations" page from the University of Manitoba (**http://www.umanitoba.ca/counselling/careers.html**). Both offer hyperlinks to pages describing dozens of occupations.

Some of the major online services and search tools maintain special areas for job seekers. These areas generally feature career-planning advice, job postings, résumé preparation tips, and other useful information. You may also be able to join a job-search newsgroup, participate in an online chat about how to interview well, or read messages posted by others who are in the job market.

For instance, visit Yahoo's search site and go to its employment area, which is located under the business category (**http://www.yahoo.com/Business/Employment/**). On this page, you can scroll through a variety of help-wanted classified ads, post your résumé for employers to consider, or drop into an interesting job-related online chat. Events and job openings change daily, so check back often.

Once you have narrowed your search to a particular occupation or industry, you can begin to study potential employers. If you know the names of companies in your targeted field, you can use an Internet search tool to locate their Web sites. Of course, these company sites are designed for promotion, so don't expect them to be objective sources of information. Still, you can get a good idea of what the company does, where it operates, and how it views its business situation.

Another way to locate company Web sites is through hyperlinks on the larger career Web sites such as Career-Index (**http://www.career-index.com**) and Career Mosaic (**http://www.careermosaic.com**). In some cases, the hyperlink leads to the company's regular Web site. In other cases, the hyperlink leads to a special recruitment page. As an example, if you click on the name of Canon under "Company Profiles" at the Career Mosaic site, you will be connected to Canon's employment site, where you can find their current list of job openings, company benefits, and general information.

## How to Find Job Openings

More and more job openings are being posted on the Internet—and not just for high-tech occupations. As you investigate any potential employer's Web site, look carefully for a hyperlink to that company's listing of job vacancies. These hyperlinks may be labeled "career opportunities," "recruitment," or some similar title.

As you might expect, computer makers such as Dell (**http://www.dell.com**) and Internet-based businesses such as Amazon.com (**http://www.amazon.com**) routinely post job openings on their Web sites and invite submission of electronic résumés. But you will also find a wide range of other firms recruiting applicants directly from their Web sites. The retail chain J.C. Penney (**http://www.jcpenney.com/**) and the global household products manufacturer Unilever (**http://www.unilever.com**) are just two of many employers that promote job openings on their Web pages.

Another way to find job openings on the Web is to visit virtual career fairs, where employers and job seekers meet online. As in any career fair, you can find out more about participating employers, explore their immediate and anticipated job openings, submit your résumé for consideration, and (sometimes) have an initial cyberspace interview.

Look for career fairs listed on career sites such as Monster.com (**http://www.monster.com**), on search sites such as (**http://www.yahoo.com/Business_and_Economy/Employment_and_Work/Jobs/Job_Fairs/**), and on dedicated job-fair sites such as the Virtual Job Fair (**http://www.vjf.com**).

Help-wanted classified ads and job databanks are available on a variety of Web sites. Best Jobs USA (**http://www.bestjobsusa.com**), a Web site maintained by *Employment Review* magazine, invites job seekers to search its listings of jobs by state or job category. You may also want to bookmark the career Web site maintained by the Wall Street Journal (**http://careers.wsj.com/**). Here, you can use the *Job Seek* function to search posted job openings by company, industry, job function, and location. If you choose, you can add your name to an e-mail list at this site so you will be alerted when new employers and new features become available.

Newspaper classified ads, a traditional source of leads for new jobs, are increasingly common on the Web. For example, if you live in the Boston area—or if you want to relocate there—you may want to search the Boston Globe's online employment classifieds (**http://careers.boston.com/**). You can use InfoSeek or another search tool to locate the Web sites of newspapers in specific cities. In addition, hyperlinks to leading newspapers are available at US Newspaper Links.com (**http://www.usnewspaperlinks.com**) and at News Directory, which serves as a gateway to dozens of U.S. publications (**http://www.ecola.com/news/press/na/us/**).

Some sites compile listings of help-wanted ads drawn from dozens of newspapers. One good example is the CareerPath Web site (**http://www.careerpath.com**). This site also lists job openings that have been posted on company Web sites, a time-saving feature that allows you to search job listings by state, name of employer, industry, and/or type of job.

If you want to post your résumé and invite prospective employers to find you, take time to investigate the growing number of résumé databanks available on the Internet. You can find listings of the largest databanks—as well as those that specialize in particular occupations—by checking career Web sites such as The Job Resource Center (**http://www.thejobresource.com**), which was started by students at Stanford University.

Employers that recruit online generally prefer to receive electronic résumés rather than the usual printed résumés. The next section shows how you can prepare your résumé for electronic submission to employers and databanks.

## How to Create an Electronic Résumé

Just as you are using your PC to search for employers and jobs via the Internet, a growing number of employers are using computers to store and search through all the résumés they receive from applicants. Instead of spending hours sifting through a mountain of cover letters and printed résumés, a manager can now enter a few key words or phrases to describe the required skills and qualifications for a particular job opening. In short order, the computer will bring up a listing of all the electronic résumés in the database that fit those exact specifications. Only applicants whose résumés are in the computer system will be considered for such job opportunities—which is why *you* need an electronic résumé.

If you have already created a résumé using a word-processing program, a few simple changes will get it into shape for submission to company computer systems and commercial résumé databanks. Start by opening the file containing your résumé, then saving it as a plain ASCII text file. Change the name, if you want, to distinguish this text-only version from the fully-formatted version.

Because text-only files cannot accommodate fancy fonts, be sure your résumé appears in one simple font and one font size. Remove any formatting such as boldface, underlining, and italics. Also remove justification, tables, rules, and columns. If you have tabs in your document, remove them and use the space bar to align your text. Then change every bullet to an asterisk or a lower-case letter o, as shown in Figure 3.2.

The first line of your résumé should contain only your full name. Type your street address, phone and fax numbers, and e-mail address on separate lines below your name. Next, count the number of characters in each line—and create

Roberto Cortez
5687 Crosswoods Drive
Falls Church, Virginia 22046
Home: (703) 987-0086     Office: (703) 549-6624
RCortez@silvernet.com

KEY WORDS

Financial executive, accounting management, international finance, financial analyst, accounting reports, financial audit, computerized accounting model, exchange rates, joint-venture agreements, budgets, billing, credit processing, online systems. MBA, fluent Spanish, fluent German, Excel, Access, Visual Basic, team player, willing to travel

OBJECTIVE

Accounting management position requiring a knowledge of international finance

EXPERIENCE

Staff Accountant/Financial Analyst, Inter-American Imports (Alexandria, Virginia)
March 1995 to present
o Prepare accounting reports for wholesale giftware importer, annual sales of $15 million
o Audited financial transactions with suppliers in 12 Latin American countries
o Created a computerized model to adjust for fluctuations in currency exchange rates
o Negotiated joint-venture agreements with suppliers in Mexico and Colombia
o Implemented electronic funds transfer for vendor disbursements, improving cash flow and eliminating payables clerk position

Staff Accountant, Monsanto Agricultural Chemicals (Mexico City, Mexico)
October 1991 to march 1995
o Handled budgeting, billing and credit-processing functions for the Mexico City branch
o Audited travel/entertainment expenses for Monsanto's 30-member Latin American sales force
o Assisted in launching an online computer system to automate all accounting functions

EDUCATION

MBA with emphasis in international business, George Mason University (Fairfax, Virginia), 1989 to 1991
BBA, Accounting, University of Texas (Austin, Texas) 1985 to 1989

INTERCULTURAL AND TECHNICAL SKILLS

Fluent in Spanish and German
Traveled extensively in Latin America
Excel, Access, HTML, Visual Basic

An attractive and fully formatted hard copy of this document is available upon request.

Figure 3.2. This résumé may serve as a good model for how to prepare an electronic résumé as you use the Web to find job opportunities.

a new line whenever the number of characters (including spaces) exceeds 65. This ensures that your electronic résumé will look neat when a potential employer brings it up on the screen.

Knowing that employers search their résumé databases according to key words, you should include a key word section near the top of your résumé. To do this, compile a list of nouns that describe your job-related skills and abilities. Some of these nouns may already be contained in your résumé, but you will also want to highlight them by positioning them in the key word section.

For example, depending on your work experience, you will want to include appropriate job titles (such as "supervisor" or "team leader") in the key word section. Similarly, if you have experience with a specialized area such as exchange rates, list the phrase "exchange rates" in your key word section. Be sure to highlight your full range of accomplishments, including such skills as fluency in other languages and any official certification courses you have completed.

Once you have completed work on your résumé, be sure to save it again as an ASCII plain text file. If you prepare separate electronic résumés for different employers or job openings, save those in separate ASCII files so you can easily access them when needed. To be sure that your electronic résumé looks good, copy and paste it into an e-mail message to yourself or to a friend. Once the e-mail message has been received, you will be able to spot and correct any formatting errors.

Remember that all the usual rules about writing a good résumé also apply to your electronic résumé: Showcase your strongest qualifications; summarize your work experience with an emphasis on results and achievements; mention relevant activities and talents; and use correct spelling and grammar. Above all, be honest. If you misrepresent your background, you may find yourself out of a job when your new employer finds out.

To get an idea of what other traditional and electronic résumés look like, you may want to browse the career sites, which often feature sample résumés. In addition, you can launch your news reader and access the newsgroup misc.jobs.resumes, where you will find many résumés posted.

Also seek out Web sites that offer general advice about résumés, both traditional and electronic. Among the many academic sites you can browse are the site sponsored by Purdue University (**http://owl.english.purdue.edu/Files/35.html**) and the site sponsored by the College of William & Mary (**http://www.wm.edu/csrv/career/stualum/resmdir/contents.html**)

Information about electronic résumés is also available at the Riley Guide (**http://www.dbm.com/jobguide/eresume.html**) and at Monster.com (see Figure 3.3) (**http://content.monster.com/resume/**). Both of these sites offer many helpful resources for preparing electronic résumés.

Once you have polished your electronic résumé, should you submit it to one or more résumé databanks? Uploading your résumé to be included in a larger databank of résumés is not the same as sending your résumé to a single employer's résumé database. The employer is going to keep your résumé in its proprietary computer system, to be accessed only by company personnel who are searching for applicants to fill job openings. Commercial résumé databanks, however, are open to many employers, which raises several issues for you to consider.

Be aware that submitting your résumé to a commercial databank makes your private information available to many people. If you have security concerns about publicizing your home address and phone number, you may want to omit

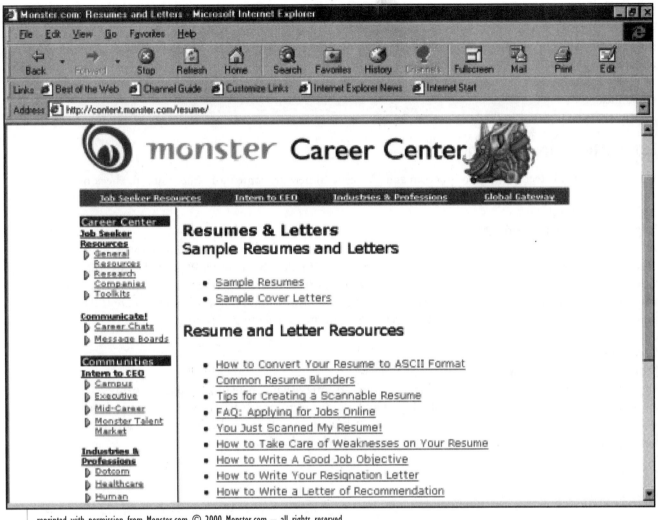

Figure 3.3. The Career Center at Monster.com offers many helpful tips on how to prepare an electronic résumé.

these details—or follow the advice of one expert, who recommends arranging for a post office box and answering service with a separate phone number to handle inquiries during the job-search period.

In addition, before you post your electronic résumé on any databank, find out who is allowed to access the résumés. Also ask whether you will be notified when an employer requests your résumé—and whether you can limit access to prevent specific organizations (such as your current employer) from requesting your résumé.

Another issue to consider is how often you are allowed to update your résumé, and whether you will be charged for doing so. At some point, you may need to correct a spelling error or add a new skill you have recently acquired. Find out whether updates are permitted and if you are expected to pay for updates. If so, continue looking until you find a suitable databank that permits free updates.

Finally, ask each commercial databank how often it removes résumés from its system. Employers want to see only up-to-date résumés, which is why some databanks get rid of older résumés after a certain number of months. So investigate the policy of any commercial databank before you submit your résumé—and, if necessary, plan to submit updated résumés at regular intervals throughout your job search.

Good luck!

## For Further Career Surfing

In addition to the career giants (Monster.com and CareerPath) here are some more career sites to check out.

### America's Job Bank
http://www.ajb.dni.us/index.html
America's Job Bank (AJB) is operated jointly by the US Department of Labor and by 1,800 local employment Service offices across the US. The listing of jobs is large (more than 950,000 jobs at last look) partly because this service provides employers with national exposure for their job listings. After searching by keywords, locations, or other options, you can get detailed descriptions of requirements, salaries, and instructions on how to apply. There is also a list of links to over 600 employer Web sites – a great way to get information about companies.

### Career Magazine
http://www.careermag.com
This site has articles on a host of job hunting topics such as interviewing, networking, and preparing resumes. There are also news items as well as calendars for job fairs and campus recruiting. Of particular interest is the searchable index of job openings. For each opening listed, you can find out details about the job, its location, the employer, and how to apply. There are also employer profiles, a resume bank, and more.

### CareerSite
http://www.careersite.com
As with most sites, job candidates can submit, free of charge, their education, skill sets, and qualifications to create an anonymous profile that can be searched by companies. The site uses something called "SmartMatch" to help you search through job listings. This search system uses "concept matching," which enables you to find better matches without having to guess the right keywords. CareerSite notifies you when employers post openings in your field. It is then up to you to send your resume.

### CareerWEB
http://www.cWeb.com
CareerWEB is mainly for professional, technical, and managerial job seekers. You can submit your resume for online access, engage in an online chat with recruiting managers, sign up to receive e-mail notification of new job openings, or view a current list of job openings by category or discipline. CareerWEB allows you to search for jobs overseas, too.

### Careers.wsj.com
http://www.careers.wsj.com
Careers.wsj.com, sponsored by the *Wall Street Journal*, is a great resource for career news and job-seeking advice, and to learn what companies are hiring for what jobs. Among the site's many features are "Career Columnists," which offers a variety of articles on career topics, and "Salaries and Profiles," which presents an in-depth review of hiring

trends and salaries nationwide. You may also use the site to be notified through e-mail about new employers and new jobs posted.

## Catapult on JobWeb
http://www.jobWeb.org/catapult

Catapult describes itself as "the springboard to career- and job-related sites that career services professionals from around the world have found helpful in working with college students and alumni." Catapult has job listings, help guides and career library resources, and cyberspace search tools. It also has links to the career offices home pages of major U.S. universities.

## College Grad Job Hunter
http://www.collegegrad.com

College Grad is a great place for juniors and seniors to get a start on life after college because it categorizes jobs as internships, entry-level positions, and experienced positions. Job seekers can link to hiring companies to find internships or full-time positions. Sample cover letters and resumes are on this site. There are also pointers for interviews and negotiation techniques.

## JOBTRAK
http://www.jobtrak.com

JOBTRAK has teamed up with over 800 college and university career centers to offer a comprehensive suite of services to both job seekers and employers. More than 3,000 new jobs are added to JOBTRAK's database each day. Students at member schools obtain a password at their school's career services office and can search the extensive listing of job openings and even sign up for online interviews. In addition, there are other extremely valuable services that don't require a password. For example, visit the page containing job search tips and resources. You'll find a first rate job search manual, tips on researching employers on the Web, and more. JOBTRAK also provides a list of its top recruiters so that job seekers can easily obtain company profiles, a guide to applying to graduate schools, and an online resume-posting service.

## Randall Hansen's Quintessential Career and Job-Hunting Resources Guide
http://www.stetson.edu/~hansen/careers

Randall Hansen is a marketing professor at Stetson University and he has put together this job resource guide. Targeted mainly at new college grads, you will find well written and detailed advice on each step of the job hunting process from evaluating your marketability, to writing a good cover letter, to writing a resume, interviewing, and locating the dream job.

## 1st Steps In The Hunt
http://www.interbiznet.com/hunt/

1st Steps helps job hunters use the Internet more effectively by publishing daily job hints, providing links to more than 4,000 companies and their job posting sites, and publishing a Recruiters Database. Tips for getting started in the job hunt, resume writing, and finding resources on the Web are provided. You can also search the top 100 electronic recruiting sites. If you post your resume, you'll receive new matching job openings by e-mail.

## 200 Letters for Job Hunters
http://www.careerlab.com/letters/

Not sure what to put in that letter to a potential employer? Mailing job search letters and no one answers? Want help writing a "thanks for the interview" latter? If so, 200 Letters for Job Hunters is divided into two parts. In part one, you will learn the "dos and don'ts" of writing a great letter. There are 239 actual letter samples divided into 20 sections. From announcing job changes, to following up, to negotiating pay, there's a sample letter that will assist in your job hunt.

## Preparing for a Career in E-Business

Start planning your career in e-business (or any business) without leaving your keyboard. The links in this section will lead you to self-assessment tools and online resources for evaluating your interests, values, and competencies and understanding your career options.

Through these self-tests and resources, you'll get a better sense of your personality, values, and goals; see how conventional jobs relate to Internet jobs; gauge your interest in applying technology and other skills; see how your values affect your career goals; and dig into your leadership potential. You'll also find more details about e-business occupations, peek inside the Internet workplace, and hone your job-search techniques.

**Personal Values Test** (on *Financial Times* site)
http://career.ft.com/CareerAdvisor/YourCareer/personalvalues_test.html
Learn more about your values and priorities by taking this in-depth self-test, posted on the careers page of the *Financial Times* Web site. The first 36 questions focus on your attitudes toward work and family relationships, your thirst for challenge and opportunity, your leadership and teamwork interests and more.

The quiz is automatically scored once you submit your answers, returning a graphical display of your answers on three dimensions (achievement, affiliation, and power). Then you're invited to read through a series of screens interpreting the questions and answers and explaining the theories behind the test material. After you answer 15 more questions about your perceptions of the job you're researching or considering, you can read more about how personal values relate to these job requirements.

**Business Interests Quiz** (on *Fast Company* Web site)
http://www.careerdiscovery.com/fastcompany/
The "Finding Your Calling" self-test, posted on the *Fast Company* magazine career pages, offers a series of questions about business-related interests, values, and abilities. These questions fall into eight general categories: using technology, working with numbers, developing theories, using creativity, counseling and mentoring, managing people, controlling resources, and influencing people through language and ideas.

Once you've clicked your way through the quiz and submitted your answers, you get back a ranking of your scores in each category, on a scale of 0 to 7 plus a brief explanation. You can use this self-assessment to gauge your interest in specific areas that apply to e-business careers, such as application of technology.

**Career Questionnaire** (on College Board Online site)
http://cbweb9p.collegeboard.org/career/html/searchQues.html
This career questionnaire from the College Board features 34 questions about your abilities, interests, temperament, and work preferences. Unlike other self-tests, this one will work even if you don't answer every question.

Once you click to submit your answers, you will see a listing of careers that match your interests and preferences. Click on each career link to see a detailed description of that job's duties, future outlook, and working conditions.

**Career Management Self-Quizzes** (on *Fortune* Career Resource Center site)
http://www.fortune.com/fortune/careers/
Follow the links on the lower part of *Fortune*'s Career Resource Center to try a number of interesting self-quizzes related to career management. Recent quizzes posted on this site include:

> What's Your Ideal Career? (Quiz focuses on interests, not aptitudes.)
> What's Your Charisma Quotient? (Quiz helps you analyze your leadership potential.)
> Is It Time to Switch Jobs? (Quiz helps you decide whether to look for another job.)
> How High Is Your Work EQ? (Quiz gauges your social skills.)
> Do You Have a Fear of Success? (Quiz examines your attitude toward success.)

**Job Hunting Quiz** (on *Career* Magazine site)
http://www.careermag.com/jobhunt_iq.html
This 16-question true-false quiz, from *Career* magazine, is a fast and easy way to see whether you've fallen victim to the "three Ms" of job hunting: misinterpretation, misunderstandings, and myths. For example, is the Internet the leading job source in terms of numbers of new employees hired? (Check the quiz to find out.)

After you click to submit your answers, you'll be shown all the right answers. The site highlights your wrong answers so you can jump directly to those sections if you prefer.

**Jobs and Dot.com Jobs** (on the Monster dot.com site)
http://dotcom.monster.com/articles/jobconverter/old.asp?jobtype=0
If you've been researching a particular job outside e-commerce and wonder how that job might apply to the online work world, this is the site for you. Simply highlight the job category that best matches the conventional job you're interested in (or qualified for), and the Job Converter shows you the equivalent job title in e-business. Then you can go on to click on links for ideas about how and where to search for that e-business job.

In addition, click to the main page at **http://dotcom.monster.com/** for job leads and more information about finding and applying for e-business positions.

**Career Key Quiz** (on the North Carolina State University site)
http://www2.ncsu.edu/unity/lockers/users/l/lkj/career_key.html
Dr. L. K. Jones developed the online Career Key quiz, which contains a series of questions about the kinds of jobs and tasks you prefer. Based on your answers, the site provides your score on six dimensions: realistic, investigative, artistic, social, enterprising, and conventional.

After your scores appear, you can browse listings of occupations well suited to each dimension. Then you can follow links to more detailed descriptions of these jobs, found in the *Occupational Outlook Handbook*.

**Career Profile Test** (on the Princeton Review site)
http://www.review.com/birkman/about_method1.cfm
The Birkman Method assess individual motivations, interests, styles, and stress behaviors to help fit the right person to the right job and the right work environment. On this site, you can click through a shortened version of the Birkman Method questionnaire by answering just 24 questions.

At the end, you'll see your score, read more about interest categories, and find a listing of suggested careers that fit your category. Then you can follow up on your own, by researching specific jobs in more detail.

**Personality Quiz** (on the PersonalityType.com site)
http://www.personalitytype.com/quiz/quiz.html
The compact quiz on this site, based on the Meyers-Briggs Type Indicator, briefly describes the four dimensions of personality and asks you to select among two alternatives for each dimension. Are you an Extravert or an Introvert? Are you a Sensor or an Intuitive? Are you a Thinker or a Feeler? Are you a Judger or a Perceiver?

Once you've made your selections, you'll see a description of your personality type, along with a listing of suggested careers to investigate. Use this test to consider how your personal preferences relate to different career choices.

## Additional Resources

Check these links for more information about e-business careers and online tools for career management:

**@Brint – Biz Tech Network page**
http://www.brint.com/jobs.htm
Articles about information technology occupations, job responsibilities and salaries, required education, certification, advancement and more, plus multiple links to job and résumé sites.

**Job Briefcase self-test page**
http://jobbriefcase.com/tips/tests.htm
On this site, you can take several brief self-tests about preparing for the job search, job-search skills, and personal strengths and weaknesses.

**CNET Tech Jobs page**
http://jobs.cnet.com/Main/Index_m.jsp
This site contains numerous links to articles about technology careers plus downloadable self-tests to help you assess your job capabilities.

**ComputerWorld Careers page**
http://www.computerworld.com/
Look for the careers link for career articles and a searchable database of jobs in information technology.

**High Technology Careers Magazine page**
http://www.hightechcareers.com/
Articles about careers in computer technology, systems, and engineering, with tips about hottest employers, on-the-job strategies, Silicon Valley updates, and more.

**Internet Sourcebook careers page**
http://www.internetsourcebook.com/jobs/index.html
Just for e-business careers, a page with links to company job openings, job databases, industry publications and newsgroups, e-business profiles, and many other useful resources.

**Kaplan Careers page**
http://www1.kaplan.com/view/zine/0,1899,8,00.html
Here's your chance to see what a real job interview feels like—with a few clicks of your mouse—by sitting through Kaplan's "Hot Seat" mock job interview.

**Monster campus page**
http://campus.monster.com/tools/virtual/
Practice answering job-interview questions like "What do you do in your spare time?" on Monster's Virtual Interview self-test.

**Siliconvalley.com Future of Work page**
http://www.mercurycenter.com/svtech/columns/future/
Read Aryae Coopersmith's insightful columns for a peek inside the Internet as a workplace and who works there.

**The Vault Internet/new media page**
http://www.vault.com
Follow the link to the Internet/New Media page for the latest industry news, newsletters with job advice, a jobs message center, and listings of job openings.

**WebMonkey job tips page**
http://hotwired.lycos.com/webmonkey/jobs/tips/index.html
Check out these articles for practical advice about researching and landing an e-business job.

# Chapter 4
# Distance Learning on the Internet

## What is Distance Learning?

Imagine an educational system in which you can take a course, submit an assignment, even interact with your instructor and classmates without stepping into a real classroom—that's distance learning. As the name implies, students are physically separated from instructors (and often from each other) in a distance learning arrangement. The idea is to bring the learning to the student rather than bring the student to the learning, which provides more flexibility and more options for personal and professional growth.

As a student, you can participate in distance learning in a variety of ways. In some programs, you receive instruction and assignments via the Internet, using e-mail, audio streaming, video clips, group chats, or other techniques. In other programs, you watch your instructor on videotape, videoconference, or television. Your alternatives for distance learning will depend on the provider of the course you select.

Today, some form of distance learning is available at more than half of all four-year colleges and universities in the United States—and many offer degree programs entirely by Internet. For example, the Colorado Electronic Community College (**http://www.ccconline.org**) offers an Internet-only associate degree program. Similarly, the University of Phoenix (**http://www.uophx.edu/online/**) offers Internet-only undergraduate and graduate degrees. These types of programs allow students to use the Internet for almost everything, from ordering textbooks and filling out financial aid forms to downloading course materials and taking quizzes.

Distance learning is also becoming more popular at colleges and universities around the world, from the University of Leicester in the United Kingdom (**http://www.le.ac.uk/education/courses/distance.html**) to Macquarie University in Australia (**http://www.mq.edu.au/study.html**).

Colleges are not the only sources of distance learning programs. Employers have begun to embrace distance learning in its many forms. As one example, the Tennessee Valley Authority offers career enrichment courses by videotape and by self-paced computer training, in addition to its traditional classroom courses. As another example, employees of GTE Corporation can attend educational videoconferences on personal finance as well as participate in job-related courses.

Professional organizations such as the Illinois Association of Realtors are also using distance learning on the Internet to provide continuing education training to their members. And distance learning is now being developed by some companies as a profit-making venture. ZDNet University (**http://www.zdu.com**) is a good example. An offshoot of Ziff-Davis, which publishes magazines on information technology, ZDNet University offers courses on Internet technology and its business applications.

Distance is no object when you are able to access learning materials via the Internet. Whether a course originates in another city, state, or country, all students receive the same lectures, assignments, and attention. As a result, a student in the United States can sign up for an education class at the University of Birmingham, Westhill, in England (**http://www.westhill.ac.uk/w10.html**), while a student in California can log onto any course offered by Syracuse University Continuing Education OnLine in New York State (**http://www.suce.syr.edu/online/**).

Wherever you are, whatever you want to learn, you can probably find a distance learning course somewhere in the world to meet your needs.

## Advantages and Disadvantages

Distance learning on the Internet has many advantages. At the top of the list is the broad array of choices. You can earn a degree, obtain continuing education credits, sharpen your work skills, prepare for a new job or career, stay abreast of fast-changing technology, even master a new subject for personal enrichment—all without leaving your keyboard.

Easy access is another major advantage. As long as you have the right computer hardware and software as well as a connection to the Internet, you can be a distance learning student. Just log on to the course's Web site to download the latest lecture, or enter the designated chat room for a cyberspace exchange of ideas. If you have a laptop computer with modem, you can easily send in your course assignments from home, office, or almost anywhere.

Most of the time, distance learning on the Internet allows you to work at your own pace, an important advantage for people who are juggling school and work responsibilities and those whose schedules can change from day to day. Rather than having to be in the classroom at a particular time, distance learning students can usually access a Web site at any hour to read new assignments or e-mail the instructor with questions.

Distance learning on the Internet can save you money, though some undergraduate and graduate courses may be more costly than traditional classroom courses. Still, by using the Internet for distance learning, you completely avoid charges for room and board (or the cost of traveling to class), which can represent a significant savings.

Of course, distance learning on the Internet has disadvantages, as well. One key disadvantage is the lack of live interaction with the instructor and with classmates. If you thrive on classroom debate or prefer to have your questions answered immediately, you may not like having to type your comments or wait for an e-mailed response.

Some programs have addressed this issue by arranging for periodic desktop videoconferencing. Students and instructors place small video cameras on their computer monitors and speak into microphones to participate in group discussions during a desktop videoconference session. Students can see the instructor, the instructor can see the students, and everybody can hear every comment.

Of course, you must have an appropriately configured personal computer and an Internet connection to take an online course. To meet these needs, some schools are inviting their distance-learning students to use the computer facilities on campus or at regional satellite centers.

Overall, distance learning is best suited to students who are motivated to assume responsibility for their own learning. You must be willing to log onto the course Web site at regular intervals; download and review instructional materials; and post your questions or ask for additional help.

Remember, some courses require students to visit chat rooms for group discussions. Some courses mandate frequent or lengthy homework projects, while others expect students to read and comment on classmates' reports and projects. You have to be ready to invest sufficient time and effort to meet all these course requirements. You must also have the flexibility to deal with the occasional technical glitches that can crop up. Only you can decide whether distance learning is right for *you*.

## A Distance Learning Sampler

To supplement your search efforts, you may want to take a few minutes to browse the following Web sites, just a small sample of the many distance learning opportunities available on the Internet. Some of these sites contain hyperlinks to other programs or additional sources of information that can be useful as you expand your search.

### General Information

- Tips for success: how to get the most from any distance learning opportunity, from the College of DuPage, IL. http://www.dupage.edu/excel.html

- Find and evaluate college-level distance learning courses using the Distance Learning Resource Network's listing of printed and Internet resources. http://www.fwl.org/edtech/CollegeDistanceEd.html

- Browse categorized listings of hyperlinks for distance learning programs, technology providers, and sources of information about distance learning theory and technique. http://www.online.uillinois.edu/public_service/index.html

### Academic Credit

- The National Universities Degree Consortium Web site offers hyperlinks to 9 accredited universities that cooperatively offer distance learning courses for undergraduate and graduate degrees as well as certificate programs. Members include Kansas State University and Colorado State University. http://www.nudc.org/

- At the New Jersey Institute of Technology, students can complete bachelor's or master's degrees in computer science and information systems and 10 graduate certificates in their entirety via distance learning. A large number of undergraduate and graduate courses are also offered through distance learning. http://www.njit.edu/DL/

- The West Suburban Post-Secondary Chicago consortium of colleges and universities provides online access to distance learning courses through members such as College of DuPage, Illinois Institute of Technology, and North Central College. http://www.wspsc.org

- New Promise is a site that contains a comprehensive listing of distance learning courses and providers with brief descriptions plus hyperlinks to more detailed data. http://www.newpromise.com/home/

- University of Minnesota offers undergraduate degrees using a variety of distance learning techniques, including Internet-based instruction. http://www.cee.umn.edu/dis/

- Ohio University Independent Study allows students to earn credit toward undergraduate degrees using various distance learning techniques, including e-mail. http://www.cats.ohiou.edu/~indstu/index.htm

- University of Phoenix offers numerous undergraduate and graduate courses (and continuing education courses); cyberstudents can earn a bachelor's or master's degree entirely through online study. **http://www.uophx.edu/**

## Career Development

- Certificate programs in telecommunications are available through distance learning programs on the Internet from the University College of the University of Denver; students can also earn undergraduate and graduate degrees in a number of disciplines. **http://www.du.edu/ucol/tele/teleidx.html**

- The College for Financial Planning's CPE Internet (see Figure 4.1) offers a range of courses to meet continuing education requirements and enhance professional proficiency. Try a free online orientation course to preview the learning method before registering. Go to **http://www.cpeinternet.com/** and visit the "How it Works" section.

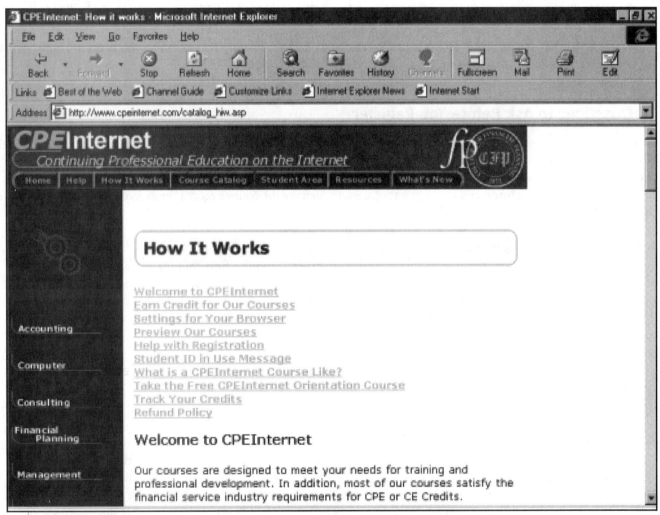

Figure 4.1. CPE Internet is one of many educational institutions offering courses on the Internet.

- The Indiana University School of Continuing Studies offers online certificate programs, credit and noncredit courses in labor studies, workforce development, and other management subjects. http://www.indiana.edu/~iude/

- Professional certificates in accounting, business, and management are offered through the Internet by Champlain College Online in Vermont; associate and bachelor's degrees are also available. http://www.champlain.edu/OLDE/index.html

### Personal Enrichment
- LearnItOnline from ZDNet (Ziff-Davis, publisher of tech magazines) offers online learning to help users get the most from programs such as Web browsers, word processing, and graphics software. http://www.learnitonline.com/

- Syracuse University Continuing Education Online offers a variety of non-credit courses, including Investing and Trading on the Internet, Grant Writing, and Textile Ergonomics. http://www.suce.syr.edu/online/

- The WhaleNet educational Web site, from Wheelock College in Boston, has everything you want to know about whales and marine life—and more. http://whale.wheelock.edu/

## 10 Questions to Ask Before You Register

No matter what goal you want to achieve by taking a distance learning course, you should ask pointed questions before making any commitments. A little advance checking will help you determine the potential benefits and value of each course under consideration. Just as important, these questions will help you recognize potential problems, eliminate inappropriate courses, and narrow your options to identify the courses most suited to your particular needs and situation.

### 1. Who is offering the course?
Find out about the institution, company, or organization offering the course. If the sponsor appears to be an educational institution, is it a real college or university (or a legitimate affiliate)? Names can be deceiving: what sounds like a prestigious university may actually be a front for a rip-off, so do some checking. Similarly, if a company or professional organization is sponsoring the course, you will want to investigate the sponsor's reputation and background before you sign a contract or send money.

The address of the Web site can often provide some clues: **.com** indicates a for-profit site, while **.edu** indicates an educational site. Also look for contact information such as the sponsor or institution's address, phone and fax numbers, affiliations, and other details.

### 2. Is the course part of an accredited program?
Accreditation is a critical issue for students seeking to earn a recognized degree. If a distance learning course is part of an unaccredited program, you may not be able to transfer the credits to an institution with an accredited program. If you are interested in pursing a degree entirely by distance learning and then continuing to study for even higher degrees, you should be sure that your diploma and coursework will be recognized by other institutions and by potential employers.

Legitimate educational institutions can provide solid information about their accreditation and refer you to the accrediting body for more details. Be especially careful about checking the accreditation of for-profit sponsors—and check on the accrediting body, as well. Accreditation is a complex topic, so you may want to talk with an administrator at a nearby college or university as an initial step.

### 3. What is the time commitment?
This is actually a two-part question. First, find out about the time requirements for an individual course. How often must students "meet" for cyberspace discussions (if ever)? How many meetings are required over the entire course? How much time is allowed for submitting assignments? How long can you expect the entire course to last? Must you log on a certain number of times or devote a given amount of time to coursework in order to obtain credit?

Second, if you are planning to take distance learning courses to earn a degree, you will want to ask how many months or years students typically need to complete all their courses and qualify for graduation. In most cases, all courses are not offered year-round, which can slow you down if you are trying to earn a degree quickly. Some institutions schedule courses more frequently, to accommodate students who are in a hurry. In addition, some institutions have regulations regarding the length of time a student can take to complete a degree, so check before you enroll.

### 4. What is the cost?
Ask about the tuition per course or per credit as well as any additional charges, such as registration or administration fees. Also ask about payment methods and schedules; nearly every school allows payment by major credit card, and some will accept payments in installments.

If textbooks or other learning materials must be purchased, take these into consideration when calculating the total cost of any distance learning course. Finally, consider the cost of dialing into the Internet to participate in the course.

### 5. What is the content?
Is the course merely an introduction to a topic—or is it an in-depth examination? Is the focus primarily on theory or will you also learn tips for practical application? Is the course covering the latest advances in the field? To answer these questions, you may have to go beyond the course description shown on the screen or in the catalog. In some cases, you will have to contact the institution or sponsoring organization to get more details about the exact content of a particular course. Then ask yourself whether you are really interested in the course content—and whether the coverage will help you meet your goals.

### 6. What are the teacher's credentials?
Although some of what you learn in an online course will come from the text—and some from the comments and suggestions of other students—you will also want to look at your teacher's qualifications. How does the teacher's educational and/or work background fit with the course content? Has the teacher had much hands-on experience in applying what is being taught? How long has the teacher been teaching this or similar courses?

Many distance learning programs invite prospective students to read brief biographies of their faculty members. Before you sign up for a course, browse the Web site to read about the teachers so you can make an informed decision.

### 7. What are the entrance requirements or prerequisites?
As with traditional college or training programs, many distance learning programs impose entrance requirements or prerequisites. For example, some online master's or doctoral programs are open only to students with extensive work

experience, just as some professional courses on the Internet are open only to those who have attained a particular standing or seniority in the industry.

Sometimes students cannot enroll in advanced courses unless they have taken lower-level courses as prerequisites. This is the case in many high-tech courses, where a basic knowledge of a particular programming language is generally required for admission. You should check on any requirements so you can plan to take courses in the appropriate order and at the appropriate point in your career.

## 8. How is the course conducted?

Before you sign up, you will want to take time to find out how your course will be conducted. Internet-based courses are often presented via a combination of e-mail, chat, electronic slide shows, and audio- or video-enhanced materials—in addition to a printed text. Some online courses may require a non-Internet component as well (such as teleconferencing).

A few schools allow students to try a sample class or course in advance. For example, Champlain College Online offers a sample course on Vermont history. Students simply sign up (**http://www.champlain.edu/OLDE/sample.htm**) and wait for e-mail instructions that explain how to log onto the system to access course materials.

As you investigate the way the course is conducted, also consider the communication between teachers and students. Are you expected to work individually or as part of a team of students to complete one or more class projects? How much e-mail interaction can you expect with the teacher? With other students? The answers to these questions will help you gauge whether a course fits your individual learning style and personal preferences.

## 9. What equipment is required?

At the very least, distance learning courses on the Internet require access to a properly configured personal computer with modem, Web browsing software, and a dial-up connection to the Internet. Individual courses may require additional software, such as a word processing program for writing reports or technical software for completing assignments.

You can usually learn about equipment requirements in advance by reading the course description or checking the school's Web site for more information. If all else fails, send an e-mail to the institution or sponsor to inquire about the necessary equipment.

## 10. What assistance is available—and when?

In distance learning, students bear most of the responsibility for successful learning. However, there will be times when you decide to seek assistance. You may want guidance about courses; you may want help entering the Web site for a scheduled class "chat" session; or you may have some other problem or question. Some colleges and universities offer online assistance through self-guided tutorials or access to experts via e-mail. At Rogers University, for example, students can obtain academic and career counseling from student services at the school's Web site (**http://www.ruonline.edu**).

Be prepared: before you take any class, find out how and when you can obtain help. Although you may be eager to fix a problem at 2 a.m. so you can download an assignment right away, you may not be able to get help at that hour. So play it safe: ask for a name or department to contact and get a telephone number as well as an e-mail address in case you have an urgent request. You may even want to make a request to experience the help system first-hand before you register.

# Learning in Cyberspace

How does a cyberstudent actually participate in a distance learning course on the Internet? The answer depends on the format of the course—and the student's individual learning style.

In this section, you will follow along as Vicky, an undergraduate cyberstudent enrolled in the University of Phoenix's online program, participates in the first week of a five-week Organizational Behavior course. Because this course is conducted entirely via online messages, the instructor's role is particularly critical.

## The instructor's role

Chad Lewis, the instructor for this Organizational Behavior course, has been teaching online since the early days of Internet-based education. Following the University of Phoenix model, Chad carefully plans his courses to provide a distinct structure to the learning experience.

Online courses at University of Phoenix start on Thursdays, with each course divided into five week-long "workshops" covering related topics. By the time his cyberstudents dial into the school's computer system on the first Thursday of the course, Chad has already posted his initial lecture notes and assignments. He will continue to post new lecture notes and assignments every Thursday until the final week of the course.

Throughout the five weeks, Chad goes online several times each day to read student messages, respond to their comments, and help those who have questions about the coursework or the mechanics. His written syllabus lets students know exactly when their assignments are due; he also requires class "participation"—students must read their classmates' answers and reports, then post responses. By sticking to an established timetable and maintaining an online active presence, Chad adds structure to the learning process—the online equivalent of attendance in a regularly scheduled class in a physical school facility.

In addition, Chad carries on a private e-mail correspondence with each student. (Students can also call or fax instructors with any questions or concerns.) By noon on Saturdays, Chad makes it a point to have all homework graded and returned to his students' private mailboxes. This feedback allows students to track their progress. "In an online environment, instructors can never give students too much feedback," he says. "Students need to know how they are doing and what is expected of them."

## Getting ready for class

Before Vicky can attend online classes at the University of Phoenix, she must apply for admission, register for each course, receive confirmation of acceptance into the class, install special software for class communication, and order the course materials (in this case, a textbook, a book of supplementary readings, and a course curriculum). Students are expected to log onto the class meeting at least five out of seven days so they can read messages and post responses. Because the coursework is so intense, students are allowed to take only one five-week class at a time.

When Vicky launches the school's software and logs onto the system Thursday morning, she finds two messages from Chad, her instructor. One contains his biography, with the request that students upload their own biographies to the class meeting as soon as possible.

The second message presents the course syllabus, with the content and assignments for each of the five week-long workshops. From that message, Vicky learns that each week-long workshop will follow a particular schedule:

- Thursday: The instructor posts a new lecturette in the "class meeting" section of the online system.
- Saturday: After reading the corresponding text materials, students upload answers to questions posed in the lecturette.
- Sunday: Students prepare either a case analysis or a short report and upload it to the "cases and reports" section of the online system.
- Wednesday: Students write and submit a brief summary of the most meaningful learning experiences gained from that week's workshop, including an analysis of how they can apply the knowledge in their work life.

After the first week, Vicky will be sure to check her private e-mailbox every Saturday for graded homework returned (with comments) by the instructor. Once she downloads and prints the syllabus and the first week's lecturette, she is ready to participate in the first workshop.

## Class is in session
With syllabus in hand, Vicky is ready for the first week of the course.

### Thursday
When Vicky comes home from work on Thursday, she writes a one-page biography, and logs on to upload this message to the class meeting. Already, 5 of the 12 students have posted their biographies. Todd is an engineer working in Cleveland; Amelia is a nurse who has just moved to San Diego; Curtis is interviewing for a new manufacturing job in Houston; Roberto is a systems analyst in Nashville; and Cindy is an assistant manager in a Boston store.

Vicky notices that Roberto has also posted a message for Curtis, asking whether any students from their previous online class will be in the Organizational Behavior class. To break the ice, Vicky posts a message for Todd, introducing herself and asking whether he knows her cousin, who works in Cleveland. Then she logs off, reads the lecturette, and starts reading the first of the two chapters required for that week's workshop, which focuses on the nature and functions of management.

Late Thursday evening, Vicky logs on again and downloads the biographies of four more students. She also finds a message from Todd, who doesn't know her cousin but does share her interest in baseball. Vicky posts a brief message for Chad, the instructor, to ask about the textbooks he has written. Then she logs off, ending her first day in that week's workshop.

### Friday
At dinnertime on Friday, Vicky goes online to download the biographies of the last two students. Three other students have posted messages commenting on Vicky's biography and asking a question or two about her background. Chad has posted a response to Vicky's question (as well as responses to two other students' comments or questions).

Later that evening, Vicky finishes reading the second chapter in the textbook and the two supplemental readings. Then she logs on to the class meeting and reads the messages from the students who have posted their answers to the instructor's questions.

### Saturday
On Saturday morning, Vicky rereads the lecturette questions. Then she drafts her answers, logs onto the system, and uploads her work. Next, she reads through all the other students' answers—making notes as she reads—then types her response to each. She questions one student's defense of scientific management, but agrees with another that total quality management is a key competitive tool, based on her company's experience in the global marketplace.

Later that day, Vicky writes a first draft of her case analysis, citing sources in the text and the supplemental readings. If she wants to look for extra sources to supplement the text, she can tap into the search facilities of the University of Phoenix's Web-based library resource.

## Sunday

By mid-day Sunday, Vicky is back at her computer, putting the finishing touches on her case analysis. She logs onto the system, uploads this assignment, and then reads all the new messages. This is the fourth day of the workshop, and she has read through nearly 100 messages posted in the class meeting.

Reading and responding to her classmates' messages takes time, but the process gives Vicky a more in-depth understanding of the concepts and their application to real-world situations. In fact, as she reads the comments posted by other students, Vicky begins to rethink her own answers.

## Tuesday

Although she is too busy on Monday to log on to the class meeting, Vicky goes online early Tuesday morning to read more messages and to respond to her classmates' comments about her case analysis. Some agree with her ideas, citing their own reading and on-the-job experiences, while some argue for a slightly different approach. Chad has responded to some of the student comments, as well. Rather than respond immediately, Vicky prints the messages and logs off to read them more carefully. Then, before dinner, she goes online again to post her responses and read the next batch of messages posted by her classmates.

## Wednesday

On Wednesday morning, Vicky checks the class meeting for any last-minute postings. Then she logs off and makes notes for her summary of the most meaningful learning experiences gained from the first weekly workshop. At the top of her list is her new awareness of the diversity of functions that a manager in any organization must perform. Next, she writes about the lively debate over scientific management—and her belief that creative, empowered employees are the essential ingredient in peak organizational performance. She ends her summary with a commitment to developing her own conceptual skills, since her attention to detail sometimes obscures the big picture.

Logging on before dinner to upload her summary, Vicky takes a few minutes to read what other students have posted. After typing a few messages in response, she logs off for the day. The second week-long workshop begins the next day, and Vicky wants to read ahead in preparation for the lecturette that will be posted in the class meeting on Thursday. It has been an intense week, but Vicky has enjoyed all the interaction with her classmates, and she is looking forward to her instructor's comments on the homework assignment, which will be returned to her private e-mailbox on Saturday.

## Class is over

During the fifth week of this Organizational Behavior course, Vicky downloads the final exam that Chad has posted in the class meeting. At this point, she has completed all the assignments and read through every online message posted by the instructor and the students. After she uploads the integrative report that serves as her final exam, she will wait a few days to find her final grades in her private e-mailbox—then the course will be over.

In addition to absorbing the basic concepts and thinking about their application to real work situations, Vicky has benefited from the insights offered by her diverse group of classmates. Although she has never actually seen Chad or any of her classmates, she feels as though she knows them through their online messages. Just as important, she was able to take the entire course without disrupting her ordinary work schedule, one of the key benefits of distance learning on the Internet.

# Chapter 5
# Business—Related Internet Addresses

E-commerce, job searches, distance learning... It's all happening over the Internet. So you'll likely be spending more and more time at the keyboard. To help you get where you want to go, we're providing some important Internet addresses. This list of business-related URLs is a great jumping-off point for your business information needs. From actual company home pages to government resources to discipline-specific sites, give these URLs a try.

| Site Name/Sponsor | Address |
|---|---|
| **Accounting** | |
| Rutgers University | http://www.rutgers.edu/Accounting/ |
| Edgar | http://www.sec.gov.edgarhp.htm |
| Edgar-Online | http://www.edgar-online.com/ |
| American Accounting Association | http://www.rutgers.edu/Accounting/raw/aaa/ |
| American Institute of Certified Public Accountants | http://ww.rutgers.edu/Accounting/raw/aicpa/home.htm |
| **Businesses** | |
| 3M Dental Products Division | http://www.mmm.com/dental/baldrige |
| 3M Innovation Network | http://www.mmm.com |
| ADAC Laboratories | http://www.adaclabs.com |
| Aetna | http://www.aetna.com |
| American Express | http://www.americanexpress.com |
| American Society for Quality | http://www.asq.org |
| American Stock Exchange | http://www.amex.com |
| Ameritech | http://www.ameritech.com |
| Analog Devices | http://www.analog.com |
| Armstrong World Industries | http://www.armstrong.com |
| AT&T | http://www.att.com |
| Australian Quality Council | http://www.aqc.org.au |
| Avis | http://www.avis.com |
| BASF | http://www.basf.com |
| Bell Atlantic | http://www.bell-atl..com |
| Black & Decker | http://www.blackanddecker.com |
| Boise Cascade Corporation | http://www.bc.com |
| Bureau of Labor Statistics | http://stats.bls.gov |
| Canon | http://www.usa.canon.com |
| CBS Corporation | http://www.cbs.com |
| Charles Schwab & Co. | http://www.schwab.com |

| | |
|---|---|
| Cisco | http://www.cisco.com |
| Citicorp | http://www.citibank.com |
| Coca-Cola | http://www.coca-cola.com |
| Compaq Computer Corporation | http://www.compaq.com |
| Corning | http://www.corning.com |
| DaimlerChrysler | http://www1.daimlerchrysler.com |
| Dana Corporation | http://www.dana.com |
| Deming Institute | http://deming.org/ |
| DuPont | http://www.dupont.com |
| Eli Lilly | http://www.lilly.com |
| Eastman Chemical | http://www.eastman.com |
| Federal Express | http://www.fedex.com |
| Fidelity Investments | http://www.fidelity.com |
| Florida Power & Light Company | http://www.fplgroup.com |
| Ford Motor Company | http://www.ford.com |
| General Electric Corporation | http://www.ge.com |
| General Motors Corporation | http://www.gm.com |
| Granite Rock | http://www.graniterock.com |
| GTE Corporation | http://www.gte.com |
| Hershey Foods | http://www.hersheys.com |
| Hewlett-Packard | http://www.hp.com |
| Home Depot | http://www.homedepot.com |
| Honda Motor Co., Inc. | http://www.honda.com |
| IBM Rochester | http://www.ibm.com/ |
| Intel Corporation | http://www.intel.com |
| John Deere & Co. | http://www.deere.com |
| Juran Institute | http://www.juran.com |
| Kodak | http://www.kodak.com |
| L.L. Bean | http://www.ll.bean |
| Lotus | http://www.lotus.com |
| MCIWorldcom | http://www.mciworldcom.com |
| Marlow Industries | http://www.marlow.com |
| Marriott Corporation | http://www.marriott.com |
| Mazda Motor Corporation | http://www.mazda.com |
| MBNA Corporation | http://www.mbnainternational.com |
| Merrill Lynch Credit Corporation | http://www.ml.com |
| Microsoft | http://www.microsoft.com |
| Milliken & Co. | http://www.milliken.com |
| Motorola | http://www.mot.com |
| NCR Corporation | http://www.ncr.com |
| New York Life Insurance Co. | http://www.newyorklife.com |
| Nissan Motors | http://www.nissan.co.jp |
| NIST Quality Program (Baldridge) | http://www.quality.nist.gov |
| Novell | http://www.novell.com |
| Nucor Corporation | http://www.nucor.com |
| PepsiCo, Inc | http://www.pepsico.com |
| Philip Crosby and Associates | http://www.philipcrosby.com |

| | | |
|---|---|---|
| | Proctor & Gamble | http://www.pg.com |
| | Quality Digest Magazine | http://www.qualitydigest.com |
| | Raytheon | http://www.raytheon.com |
| | Siemens | http://www.siemens.de/en |
| | Solectron Corporation | http://www.solectron.com |
| | Southwest Airlines | http://www.iflyswa.com |
| | Sun Microsystems, Inc. | http://www.sun.com |
| | Texas Instruments | http://www.ti.com |
| | Toyota Motor Corporation | http://www.toyota.co.jp |
| | Trident Precision Manufacturing, Inc. | http://www.tridentprecision.com |
| | Unisys | http://www.unisys.com |
| | UPS | http://www.ups.com |
| | Walt Disney Company | http://www.disney.com |
| | Whirlpool Corporation | http://www.whirlpool.com |
| | Xerox Corporation | http://www.xerox.com |
| | Zenith Data Systems | http://www.zds.com |
| | Zytec Corporation | http://www.zytec.com |
| **Business Law** | | |
| | Legal Information Institute | http://www.law.cornell.edu/ |
| | Ray August – Professor of Business Law | http://august1.com |
| | ABA Lawlink | http://www.abanet.org/lawlink/home.html |
| | Law Resources on the Internet | http://www.rbvdnr.com/lawres.htm |
| **Business Publications** | | |
| | Inc. Magazine | http://www.inc.com |
| | Dow Jones | http://dowjones.wsj.com |
| | Electronic Newsstand | http://www.enews.com |
| **Business Statistics** | | |
| | SPSS | http://www.spss.com |
| | Statistics on the Web | http://www.execpc.com/~helberg/statistics.html |
| | Basic Sources of Economic Statistics | http://www.princeton.edu/~econlib/basic.html |
| **Finance/ Economics** | | |
| | Woodrow Federal Reserve Bank of Minneapolis | http://woodrow.mpls.frb.fed.us |
| | Edgar Database of Corporate Information | http://www.sec.gov/edgarhp.htm |
| | Dunn & Bradstreet | http://www.dnb.com |
| | Money Magazine Personal Finance Center | http://www.money.com/money |
| | Corporate Finance Network | http://www.corpfinet.com |
| | Hoovers Online | http://www.hoovers.com |
| | The U.S. Tax Code Online | http://www.fourmilab.ch/ustax/ |
| | PC Quote | http://www.pcquote.com |
| | Investor Web | http://www.investorweb.com |

| | |
|---|---|
| MIT Stock Master | http://www.stockmaster.com |
| Chicago Mercantile Exchange | http://www.cme.com/index.html |
| The Syndicate | http://www.moneypages.com/syndicate |
| FinanceNet | http://www.financenet.gov |
| Wall Street Journal Money & Investing Update | http://www.wsj.com |

**General Reference**

| | |
|---|---|
| List of American Universities | http://www.clas.ufl.edu/CLAS/ |
| AT&T Directory | http://www.att.net/find/index.html |
| CNN Financial Network Reference Desk | http://cnnfn.com/resources/reference |
| Better Business Bureau | http://www.bbb.org |
| The List | http://thelist.internet.com |
| Mondaq Business Briefing | http://www.mondaq.com |
| Dun & Bradstreet | http:///www.dnb.com |

**Government Resources**

| | |
|---|---|
| Library of Congress | http://www.lcweb.loc.gov/ |
| National Technology Transfer Center | http://iridium.nttc.edu/nttc.html |
| U.S. Patent & Trademark Office | http://www.uspto.gov |
| U.S. Dept. of Commerce | http://204.193.246.62/public.nsf |
| F.E.D. Resource Library | http://www.fed.org/resrclib/resrclib.htm |
| Central Intelligence Agency | http://www.odci.gov |
| Census Bureau | http://www.census.gov |

**Human Resources**

| | |
|---|---|
| AFL-CIO | http://www.aflcio.org/ |
| American Compensation Association | http://www.acaonline.org/ |
| Americans with Disabilities Act (ADA) Document Center | http://janweb.icdi.wvu.edu/kinder/ |
| Benefits Link | http://www.benefitslink.com/index.shtml |
| Career Mosaic | http://www.careermosaic.com/ |
| HR Magazine | http://www.shrm.org/docs/Hrmagazine.html |
| Training Net | http://www.trainingnet.com/ |
| Thunderbird School of International Management | http://www.t-bird.edu/ |

**Management**

| | |
|---|---|
| Institute of Management & Administration | http://www.ioma.com |
| Academy of Management | http://www.aom.pace.edu |
| Small Business Administration | http://www.sbaonline.sba.gov/ |
| International Institute for Management Development | http://www.imd.ch/ |

**Marketing**

| | |
|---|---|
| U.S. Census Bureau | http://www.census.gov |
| American Demographics Magazine | http://www.marketingtools.com |
| Nielsen Media Research | http://www.nielsen.com |
| SRI Business Intelligence Center | http://future.sri.com |

| | | |
|---|---|---|
| | Advertising Age | http://www.adage.com/ |
| | Adweek Online | http://www.adweek.com/ |
| | American Association of Advertising Agencies | http://www.aaaa.org |
| | Web Digest for Marketers | http://www.wdfm.com/ |

**Operations Management**

| | | |
|---|---|---|
| | Operations Research | http://www.rrz.uni-koeln.de/Themen/or/ |
| | Operations Research Resources | http://mat.gsia.cmu.edu/resource.html |

**Organizational Behavior**

| | | |
|---|---|---|
| | The Keirsey Temperament Sorter | http://www.keirsey.com/cgi-bin/keirsey/newkts.cgi |
| | Entrepreneur Magazine | http://www.entrepreneurmag.com/ |
| | BPR Online Learning Center | http://www.prosci.com/index.htm |
| | Psychology Centre | http://server.bmod.athabascau.ca/html/prtut/reinpair.htm |

**Small Business Management**

| | | |
|---|---|---|
| | Small Business Administration | http://www.sbaonline.sba.gov |
| | FranNet | http://www.frannet.com |
| | Institute of Management and Administration | http://www.ioma.com/index.html |
| | Franchise Handbook Online | http://www.franchise1.com/ |
| | Research Network World M & A Network | http://www.worldm-anetwork.com/ |
| | Resources for the Entrepreneur | http://www.DraperVC.com/Resources.html |

**Student Success**

| | | |
|---|---|---|
| | Tripod | http://www.tripod.com |
| | JobTrak | http://www.jobtrak.com |
| | Career Magazine | http://www.careermag.com |
| | The Accounting.com Home Page | http://www.accounting.com |
| | Job Hunter | http://www.collegegrad.com/ |
| | The Monster Board | http://www.monster.com |
| | Career Mosaic | http://www.careermosaic.com |
| | Occupational Outlook Handbook | http://stats.bls.gov:80/ocohome.htm |
| | America's Job Bank | http://www.ajb.dni.us/ |
| | HRS Federal Job Search | http://www.hrsjobs.com |

# Glossary

**advanced planning and scheduling (APS) system**  a computerized system that helps businesses evaluate varying input levels to plan for optimum production efficiency

**application service provider (ASP)**  a business that rents application software via the Internet (or via telecommunications networks) in exchange for usage or monthly fees

**auction pricing**  pricing method in which buyers bid against each other and the highest bidder buys the product

**B2B**  business-to-business transactions

**B2B (business-to-business) online markets**  Web sites that facilitate the exchange of goods and services among organizational buyers and sellers

**B2C**  business-to-consumer transactions

**B2G**  business-to-government transactions

**C2B**  consumer-to-business transactions

**C2C**  consumer-to-consumer transactions

**C2G**  consumer-to-government transactions

**cashless society**  world in which plastic or other cashless payment alternatives replace currency

**cookies**  stored information placed on consumers' hard drives to track their Internet usage

**corporate portal**  a comprehensive internal Web site with company information that employees can personalize and access as needed

**cybersquatting**  the practice of claiming a domain name with the intention of reselling it at a profit

**dynamic pricing**  method of pricing in which prices change from transaction to transaction

**e-business**  the combination of business processes, technology, and organizational structure needed for e-commerce

**e-commerce**  exchange transactions (such as buying and selling goods, services, and information) that take place on the Internet

**e-procurement**  purchasing via the Internet

| | |
|---|---|
| **e-tailers** | Internet retailers |
| **electronic barter (e-barter)** | an electronic system of barter |
| **electronic cash (e-cash)** | an electronic substitute for cash |
| **enterprise resource planning (ERP) systems** | sophisticated computer systems that allow comprehensive planning and control of operations throughout the supply chain |
| **extranet** | a private computer network available to authorized users outside the organization |
| **for-profit incubator** | a business that provides entrepreneurs with office space, business services, and management resources, as well as funding, in exchange for an equity stake |
| **G2B** | government-to-business transactions |
| **G2C** | government-to-consumer transactions |
| **G2G** | government-to-government transactions |
| **group buying** | pricing method in which the price goes down as more buyers band together to buy an item |
| **initial public offering (IPO)** | the process a company follows to sell stock to the public for the first time |
| **Internet telephony** | the transmission of telephone voice conversations via the Internet |
| **intranet** | an organization's internal computer network based on Internet technology |
| **legacy business** | a traditional, non-Internet business unit |
| **marketspace** | an electronic marketplace |
| **name-your-price strategy** | pricing strategy in which buyers state how much they will pay and suppliers decide whether to sell at that price |
| **new economy** | the economy consisting of businesses that generate all or some of their revenues from the Internet or related goods and services |
| **nexus** | a physical presence, such as a store, used in determining the tax status of a sales transaction |
| **offering price** | the price paid by investors who receive an allocation of IPO shares just before the stock starts to trade |

| | |
|---|---|
| **online catalogue** | a Web-based presentation of product information similar to a printed catalogue |
| **open text search** | a search technique in which someone enters a word or group of words for the search engine to use in scanning the Internet |
| **opt in** | asking to join an e-mail subscriber list |
| **opt out** | asking to be removed from an e-mail subscriber list |
| **profiling** | tracking consumers' online activities and using the data to create a profile of each person's interests |
| **spam** | unsolicited e-mail messages, also called junk e-mail |
| **spammer** | someone who sends junk e-mail without the audience's consent |
| **subject tree** | an online catalog of a great number of pages on the Web, organized by categories and sub-categories |
| **venture capitalists (VCs)** | investment specialists who provide funding for businesses (ventures) with high, rapid growth potential |
| **viral marketing** | the use of e-mail messages that encourage recipients to send the message to others |
| **virtual organization** | an organizational structure in which people (employees and, sometimes, non-employees) in different locations use communication technology to work together |
| **virtual teams** | teams that use technology to link members in different places |
| **virtual team leader** | person who coordinates the activities of virtual team members |

# Sources

Sources for Chapter 1 Introduction:

Robert D. Hof, "Shoppers: Take Charge," *Business Week*, May 15, 2000, EB 130; Irene M. Kunii, "Architects: Keiichi Enoki, DoCoMo," Business Week, May 15, 2000, EB 44; Keith Regan, "Report: Q1 E-Commerce Matches Holiday Pace," *E-Commerce Times*, May 1, 2000, http://www.ecommercetimes.com/news/articles2000/000501-3.shtml; Virginie Robert, "Who Will Be the Amazons of Europe?" *Connectis*, February 25, 2000, http://www.ft.com; "Define and Sell," *The Economist*, February 26, 2000, E-Commerce sec., 6, 11-15; "Something Old, Something New," *The Economist*, February 26, 2000, E-Commerce sec., 15-24; "I-Modest Success," *The Economist*, March 11, 2000, 69-70; Keith Perine, "Making City Hall Obsolete," *The Standard.com*, March 13, 2000, http://www.thestandard.com; Robert Conlin, "European E-Commerce Poised For Boom," *E-Commerce Times*, March 28, 2000, http://www.ecommercetimes.com/news/articles2000/000328-7.shtml; "Internet Economics: A Thinkers' Guide," *The Economist,* April 1, 2000, 64-66; "E-Mail Continues To Take Over the World," *Internet.com*, April 4, 2000, http://www.cyberatlas.internet.com; "New Study Finds Many E-Retailers Won't Last," *News-Times (Danbury, CT)*, April 13, 2000, A14; Jon Caramanica, "The C2G Portal Play," *Wired*, April 2000, 86; "Efficiency.Gov," *Business 2.0*, April 2000, 56; Efraim Turban, Jae Lee, David King, and H. Michael Chung, *Electronic Commerce: A Managerial Perspective* (Upper Saddle River, N.J.: Prentice Hall, 2000), 4-5; Vanessa Richardson, "GovWorks Receives VC Vote," *Redherring.com*, November 8, 1999, http://www.redherring.com; Ravi Kalakota and Marcia Robinson, *E-Business: Roadmap for Success* (Reading, MA: Addison Wesley Longman, 1999), xvi.

Sources for Marketing module:

Timothy M. Laseter, Patrick W. Houston, Joshua L. Wright, Juliana Y. Park, "Amazon Your Industry: Extracting the Value From the Value Chain," *Strategy and Business*, First Quarter 2000, http://www.strategy-business.com/strategy/00109/page1.html; Joshua Wilner, "E-Commerce Success Story: Reel.com," *E-Commerce Times*, n.d., http://www.ecommercetimes.com/success_stories/success-reel.shtml; Alice Z. Cuneo, "Sears Will Expand Sales to Retooled Hispanic Site," *Advertising Age*, October, 1999, http://www.adage.com; Chet Dembeck and Andy Wang, "Excite@Home Adds Blue Mountain To Its Arsenal, *E-Commerce Times*, October 25, 1999, http://www.ecommercetimes.com; Anne Granfield, "E-Marriage," *Forbes*, January 21, 2000, http://www.forbes.com; Penelope Patsuris, "Attention Shoppers," Forbes, January 25, 2000, http://www.forbes.com; Ralph F. Wilson, "The Six Simple Principles of Viral Marketing," *Web Marketing Today*, February 1, 2000, http://www.emarketer.com/enews/031300_viral.html; "Valentine's Day Prompts Surge in Web Traffic," *Reuters*, February 14, 2000, http://www.emarketer.com/enews/021400_rValentine.html; "Financial Journalism: Paper Wars," *The Economist*, February 19, 2000, 61-62; Dick Satran, "Sun's Shooting Star," *Business 2.0*, February 2000, 51-53; "Saturday Morning Syndrome," *The Economist*, February 26, 2000, E-Commerce sec., 37; "Sears, Bob Vila to Form Online Joint Venture to Create Definitive Home Improvement Site," Sears news release, March 3, 2000, http://www.sears.com; "Kroger to Join Sears, Carrefour and Other Retailers in Global Online Supply Marketplace," Sears news release, March 28, 2000, http://www.sears.com.

Sources for Management module:

Joan O'C. Hamilton, "The Panic Over Hiring," Business Week, April 3, 2000, EB 130-132; "Three Hours with Masayoshi Son: Softbank's Grand Plan," *President Online*, November 1999, http://www.president.co.jp/pre/9911/e_01_2.html; William C. Taylor, "Inspired by Work," *Fast Company*, November 1999, 200-208; Emily Fitzloff, "Portal Patrol," *Infoworld.com*, May 17, 1999, http://www.infoworld.com; Bill Roberts, "Web Portals Open Doors to One-Stop Services," HR Magazine, November 1999, http://www.shrm.org/hrmagazine/articles/1199roberts.htm; "Cyberventing: A Site for Sore Employees," *HR Magazine*, November 1999, http://www.shrm.org/hrmagazine/articles/1199cova.htm; Bill Leonard, "Cyberventing," *HR Magazine*, November 1999, http://www.shrm.org/hrmagazine/articles/1199cov.htm; "Rising Son," *Business Week*, January 10, 2000, 63.

Sources for Strategy module:

Karen Lake, "Interview with Cliff Sharples, CEO, Garden.com," Strategy Week, April 4, 2000, http://www.strategyweek.com; Gene G. Marcial, "Steam for Hoover's," *Business Week*, February 28, 2000, 171; Karen Lake, "Interview with Patrick Spain, Chairman and CEO, Hoover's Inc.," *Strategy Week*, February 19, 1999, http://www.strategyweek.com; "Hoover's," *Hoover's Online*, April 4, 2000, http://www.hoovers.com; "Egghead.com 2000 Sales May Rise 50%; Sees 2002 Profit," *Boston Herald*, November 23, 1999, http://www.businesstoday.com/techpages/egg11231999.htm; Kevin Ferguson, "Onsale.com and Egghead.com Combine," *Forbes*, October 6, 1999, http://www.forbes.com; Tom Davey, "What Were Those Eggheads Thinking?" *Redherring.com*, July 15, 1999, http://www.redherring.com/insider/1999/0715/news-egghead.html; Gary L. Neilson, Bruce A. Pasternack, and Albert J. Viscio, "Up the (E) Organization!" *Strategy and Business*, First Quarter 2000, http://www.strategy-business.com/strategy/00106/page1.html; Diane Brady, "How Barnes & Noble Misread the Web," *Business Week*, February 7, 2000, 63; "Something Old, Something New," *The Economist*, February 26, 2000, E-Commerce sec., 15, 18.

Sources for Finance module:

Sarah Lai Stirland, "Who Will Incubate the Incubators?" *Redherring.com*, April 10, 2000, http://www.redherring.com/vc/2000/0410/vc-incubator041000.html; Khanh T.L. Tran, "Avenue A, Niku Set Brisk Pace With Their Public Offerings," *Wall Street Journal Interactive*, March 1, 2000, http://www.wsj.com; "Street Buzzes About Services Firm IPO Share Boost," *Reuters*, February 25, 2000, http://www.news.cnet.com; Gracian Mack, "Niku Seeks Friday IPO," *Redherring.com*, February 23, 2000, http://www.redherring.com; Penelope Patsuris, "Easy Come, Easy Go," *Forbes*, April 30, 1999, http://www.forbes.com; Chris Kraeuter, "European Plan Helps Halt Niku Skid," *CBS MarketWatch*, April 5, 2000, http://www.cbs.marketwatch.com; Andrew Osterland, "Wall Street Wired," *CFO Magazine*, February 2000, http://www.cfonet.com; Richard A. Shaffer, "These Days, Who Isn't a Venture Capitalist?" *Fortune*, April 17, 2000, 532; Sam Williams, "Open Season: Andover.Net Pounds Gavel With Open IPO," *Upside Today*, January 19, 2000, http://www.upside.com.

Sources for Business Law module:

Richard Wolf, "States Move to Protect Online Privacy," *USA Today*, January 19, 2000, 1A, 2A; Heather Green, "Privacy: Outrage on the Web," *Business Week*, February 14, 2000, 38-40; James Gleick, "Patently Absurd," *New York Times Magazine*, March 12, 2000, 44-49; Anna Wilde Mathews, "U.S. Will Give Web Patents More Scrutiny Under New Plan," *Wall Street Journal*, March 29, 2000, http://www.wsj.com; Pamela L. Moore, "For Sale: Great Ideas, Barely Used," *Business Week*, April 3, 2000, 78, 80; Tyler Maroney, "The New Online Marketplace of Ideas," *Fortune*, April 17, 2000, 521-522; Timothy J. Mullaney, "Those Web Patents Aren't Advancing the Ball," *Business Week*, April 17, 2000, 62.

Sources for Accounting module:

Joe Firmage, "The New Math," *Business 2.0*, May 2000, 269-279; Catherine Yang, "Earth to Dot-Com Accountants," *Business Week*, April 3, 2000, 40-41; Robert J. Samuelson, "A High-Tech Accounting?" *Newsweek*, April 3, 2000, 37; Howard Gleckman, "The Great Internet Tax Debate," *Business Week*, March 27, 2000, 228-236; Nanette Byrnes and Richard A. Melcher, "Earnings Hocus-Pocus," *Business Week*, October 5, 1998, http://www.businessweek.com; Jeremy Kahn, "Presto Chango! Sales Are Huge!" *Fortune*, March 20, 2000, 90-96; Lisa Bertagnoli, "Little Consensus on Net Tax Issues As Vote Deadline Nears," *Marketing News*, March 13, 2000, 6; "SEC's Turner Asks for FASB's Help To Tackle Internet Accounting Issues," *Securities Law Weekly*, January 7, 2000, http://www.lawnewsnetwork.com.

Sources for Economics module:

Susan Kuchinskas, "Swap 'Til You Drop," *Business 2.0*, May 2000, 85-87; Paul A. Greenberg, "B2B Marketplaces Face FTC Scrutiny," *E-Commerce Times*, March 29, 2000, http://www.ecommercetimes.com; Robert D. Hof, "E-Malls for Business," *Business Week*, March 13, 2000, 32-34; Richard A. Oppel, Jr., "The Higher Stakes of Business-to-Business Trade," *New York Times*, March 5, 2000, sec. 3, 3; "Seller Beware," *The Economist*, March 4, 2000, 61-62; "E-Cash 2.0," The Economist, February 19, 2000, 67-69; "Cash Remains King," *The Economist*, February 19, 2000, 21; Philip Kotler, *Marketing Management* 10th edition (Upper Saddle River, N.J.: Prentice Hall, 2000), 9; "What Are the Internet Economy Indicators?" *Center for Research on Electronic Commerce*, (n.d.), http://www.internetindicators.com; Susan Moran, "Cash-Free Economy," *Business 2.0*, February 2000, 40-45.

Sources for Business Communication module:

Amy Gahran, "Major Corporate Web Contender: IBM," *Contentious*, January 6, 2000, http://www.contentious.com; Amy Gahran, "A Primer for Print Writers: How Online Is Different," *Content Spotlight*, January 31, 2000, http://www.content-exchange.com; Pat Regnier, "Why Your Broker Hates E-Mail," *Money*, October 1999, 154-156; Maxine Lans Retsky, "Spam Getting Trickier For Marketers to Use," *Marketing News*, March 13, 2000, 13; John Sanko, "Senate 'Spam' Bill Cooks Up Debate Over E-Mail," *Rocky Mountain News*, March 17, 2000, http://www.insidedenver.com/legislature/0317email.shtml.

Sources for MIS module:

Stephen Baker, "Europe Swoons for Voice-On-the-Net," *Business Week*, May 1, 2000, 196; Steve Rosenbush, "The Talking Internet," *Business Week*, May 1, 2000, 174-188; Wylie Wong, "E-Commerce Customers Chatty With Sites That Talk," CNET News, April 24, 2000, http://www.cnetnews.com; Michelle V. Rafter, "Back to the Future: San Diego's Scripps Health Is Reinventing Patient Care With a $75 Million Network Linking Doctors and Hospitals," *TheStandard.com*, April 3, 2000, http://www.thestandard.com; Corey Grice, "Phone Giants May Gain Most From ASP Market," *CNET News*, March 15, 2000, http://www.cnetnews.com; Kim Girard, "The Battle Over Renting Software," *CNET News*, February 1, 2000, http://www.cnetnews.com; "Internet Voice Comes to Online Customer Service," *E-Commerce Times*, January 31, 2000, http://www.ecommercetimes.com/news/articles2000/000131-3.shtml; Kathleen Ohlson, "New Extranet To Help NYSE Members Execute Orders Faster," *ComputerWorld*, March 17, 2000, http://www.computerworld.com; Matt Hamblen, "Shell Protects Brand Via Net," *ComputerWorld*, January 10, 2000, http://www.computerworld.com; Melanie Austria Farmer and Kim Girard, "Is the Enterprise Resource Planning Market Dead?" *CNET News*, January 4, 2000, http://www.cnetnews.com.

Sources for Decision Sciences module:

Dana Janes, "Request for Cash," *Marketing News*, March 27, 2000, 11; "Internet Enhances RFP/RFQ Process," *Purchasing*, February 10, 2000, 105; "Cincom Lights Up Fern-Howard with Manage: Enterprise," Cincom Systems, August 16, 1999, http://www.cincom.com; Ira Sager, "Big Blue Gets Wired," *Business Week*, April 3, 2000, EB 99-100; Scott Leibs, "Think Before You Link," *Industry Week*, April 17, 2000, 23+; George Taninecz, "Value Chain IT Infrastructure," *Industry Week*, April 17, 2000, 32+; Dimitry Elias Léger, "Smokestack Lightning: Eaton Hits the Web," *Fortune*, April 17, 2000, 522, 526; Ed Hess, "Make Advanced Planning and Scheduling Work For Your Company," *Integrated Solutions*, April 2000, http://www.integratedsolutionsmag.com/articles/2000_04/000408.htm.